Statistics
&
Probability

Author: Myrl Shireman

Editor: Mary Dieterich

Proofreaders: April Albert and Margaret Brown

COPYRIGHT © 2018 Mark Twain Media, Inc.

ISBN 978-1-62223-703-6

Printing No. CD-405026

Mark Twain Media, Inc., Publishers
Distributed by Carson-Dellosa Publishing LLC

Visit us at www.carsondellosa.com

Table of Contents

Table of Contents (cont.)

STATISTICS

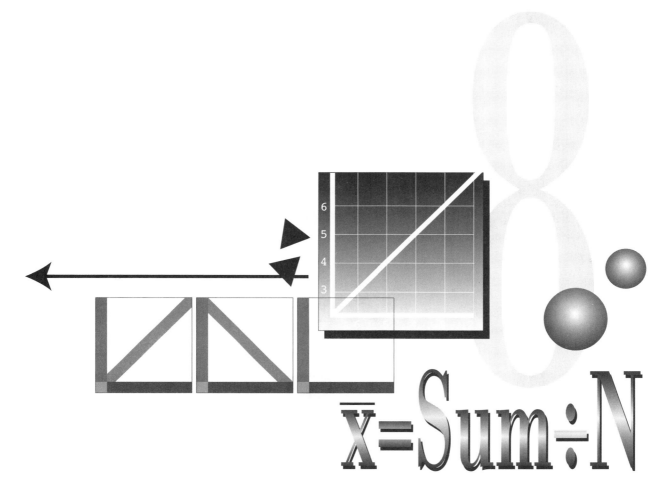

Introduction

The study and understanding of statistics is becoming increasingly important in middle-school education. The use of statistics is no longer confined to those in a few select occupations. Statistics has come to the front as one of the vital skills needed to function on the factory floor as well as in the corporate office.

This activity book is designed to introduce the student to the world of probability and statistics. The terms used are the statistical terms middle-school students must become familiar with as they prepare to continue their study of mathematics.

The worksheets are designed to give the student ample opportunity to develop a basic understanding of statistics. Many of the exercises are designed to allow students to organize and interpret data, which are skills so necessary to gaining an understanding of statistics. Other exercises are designed primarily for practice in working with common probability and statistic concepts.

The use of these exercises following a teacher-directed lesson can enhance the students' understanding of the role of statistics in today's world. Teachers are encouraged to make copies and transparencies for guided and independent practice.

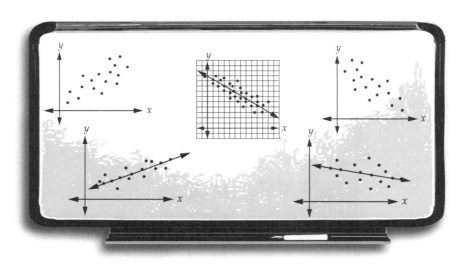

Name:_____ Date: _____

 Understanding Proper Fractions

Before learning about probability, it is important to review proper fractions. Proper fractions are very important in the study of probability.

Proper fractions are greater than zero and less than one. A proper fraction has a numerator that is smaller than the denominator. In the proper fraction $\frac{1}{2}$, the 1 is the numerator. The 2 is the denominator. It is important to remember that in a proper fraction, the numerator is always smaller than the denominator.

Directions: In the following exercise, write the numerator in the blank beside each problem.

1. $\frac{1}{3}$ _____   2. $\frac{2}{3}$ _____   3. $\frac{3}{4}$ _____   4. $\frac{4}{5}$ _____   5. $\frac{3}{8}$ _____

6. $\frac{3}{5}$ _____   7. $\frac{1}{2}$ _____   8. $\frac{7}{8}$ _____   9. $\frac{2}{5}$ _____   10. $\frac{5}{6}$ _____

Directions: In the following exercise, write the denominator in the blank beside each problem.

11. $\frac{1}{3}$ _____   12. $\frac{2}{3}$ _____   13. $\frac{3}{4}$ _____   14. $\frac{4}{5}$ _____   15. $\frac{3}{8}$ _____

16. $\frac{3}{5}$ _____   17. $\frac{1}{2}$ _____   18. $\frac{7}{8}$ _____   19. $\frac{2}{5}$ _____   20. $\frac{5}{6}$ _____

Directions: Answer the following questions. Circle the correct answer.

21. In a proper fraction, the [numerator/denominator] is always the smaller number.

22. In a proper fraction, the [numerator/denominator] is always the larger number.

23. Proper fractions always represent a number [smaller/larger] than 1.

24. In each of the following diagrams, the shaded part equals what fraction of the whole?

   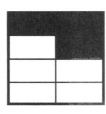   

a. _____   b. _____   c. _____

Name: _____ Date: _____

 ## Simplifying Proper Fractions

Many times it is necessary to change a proper fraction into its simplified form before finding the numerator and denominator. For example, the fraction $\frac{2}{4}$ is a proper fraction because the numerator, 2, is less than the denominator, 4. The proper fraction $\frac{2}{4}$ is not yet in its simplest form. A proper fraction is in the simplest form when the numerator and denominator are not divisible by any number other than one.

Example: To change $\frac{2}{4}$ to its simplest form, the numerator and denominator can both be divided by 2.

$$\frac{2 \text{ divided by } 2 = 1}{4 \text{ divided by } 2 = 2}$$

The proper fraction $\frac{2}{4}$ changed to its simplified form is the proper fraction $\frac{1}{2}$.

Directions: In the following exercise, change each of the proper fractions to proper fractions in simplified form.

1. $\frac{2}{6} = \dfrac{2 \text{ divided by } 2}{6 \text{ divided by } 2} = $ ____

2. $\frac{6}{10} = \dfrac{6 \text{ divided by } 2}{10 \text{ divided by } 2} = $ ____

3. $\frac{4}{6} = $ ——————— $ = $ ____

4. $\frac{5}{10} = $ ——————— $ = $ ____

5. $\frac{9}{12} = $ ——————— $ = $ ____

6. $\frac{14}{16} = $ ——————— $ = $ ____

7. $\frac{12}{15} = $ ——————— $ = $ ____

8. $\frac{4}{10} = $ ——————— $ = $ ____

9. $\frac{6}{8} = $ ——————— $ = $ ____

10. $\frac{15}{21} = $ ——————— $ = $ ____

Directions: Each of the following lines has been divided into fractional parts. Although each line is the same length and each line equals one, the fraction parts of each line are different. In these exercises, each of the fractional parts are equal. Write the fraction for each exercise over the fraction parts that make up the line. Then add the fraction parts of each line and complete the exercise.

11. $\frac{1}{5}$ $\frac{1}{5}$ $\frac{1}{5}$ $\frac{1}{5}$ $\frac{1}{5}$ $ = \frac{5}{5} = 1$

12. ____ ____ ____ ____ $ = $ —— $ = $ ___

13. ____ ____ ____ $ = $ —— $ = $ ___

14. ____ ____ ____ ____ ____ $ = $ —— $ = $ ___

15. ____ ____ ____ $ = $ —— $ = $ ___

16. ____ ____ ____ ____ ____ $ = $ —— $ = $ ___

Name:_____ Date: _____

Changing Proper Fractions to Decimals

It is often necessary to change a proper fraction to an equivalent decimal. To change a proper fraction to a decimal, the numerator is divided by the denominator. For example, the proper fraction $\frac{3}{8}$ is changed to a decimal by dividing the numerator, 3, by the denominator, 8.

Example:

$$\frac{3}{8} = 3 \div 8 = 8\overline{)3} = 8\overline{\begin{array}{r} 0.3 \\ )3.0 \\ \underline{24} \end{array}} = 8\overline{\begin{array}{r} 0.37 \\ )3.0 \\ \underline{24} \\ 60 \\ \underline{56} \end{array}} = 8\overline{\begin{array}{r} 0.375 \\ )3.0 \\ \underline{24} \\ 60 \\ \underline{56} \\ 40 \\ \underline{40} \\ 0 \end{array}} = 0.375 = 0.38 \text{ (rounded to the nearest hundredth)}$$

Directions: In the following exercise, change each of the proper fractions into decimals, using the example from above. Round each answer to the hundredths place, and place the answer in the appropriate blank.

1. $\frac{1}{3}$ = _____ = _____ = _____

2. $\frac{3}{5}$ = _____ = _____ = _____

3. $\frac{2}{3}$ = _____ = _____ = _____

4. $\frac{1}{2}$ = _____ = _____ = _____

5. $\frac{3}{4}$ = _____ = _____ = _____

6. $\frac{7}{8}$ = _____ = _____ = _____

7. $\frac{4}{5}$ = _____ = _____ = _____

8. $\frac{2}{5}$ = _____ = _____ = _____

9. $\frac{3}{8}$ = _____ = _____ = _____

10. $\frac{5}{6}$ = _____ = _____ = _____

Name:_____ Date: _____

 Changing Proper Fractions to Percents

Proper fractions are changed to percents by the following procedure:

Step 1: change the proper fraction to its decimal equivalent.

Step 2: round the decimal to the hundredths place.

Step 3: multiply the decimal by one hundred.

Step 4: write the answer followed by the percent sign.

$\frac{3}{8}$ = 0.375 = 0.38 x 100 = 38%

Directions: Solve the following problems.

	Step 1	Step 2	Step 3	Step 4
1. $\frac{1}{3}$ =	_____	0._____	0._____ x 100 = _____%
2. $\frac{3}{5}$ =	_____	0._____	0._____ x 100 = _____%
3. $\frac{2}{3}$ =	_____	0._____	0._____ x 100 = _____%
4. $\frac{1}{2}$ =	_____	0._____	0._____ x 100 = _____%
5. $\frac{3}{4}$ =	_____	0._____	0._____ x 100 = _____%
6. $\frac{7}{8}$ =	_____	0._____	0._____ x 100 = _____%
7. $\frac{4}{5}$ =	_____	0._____	0._____ x 100 = _____%
8. $\frac{2}{5}$ =	_____	0._____	0._____ x 100 = _____%
9. $\frac{3}{8}$ =	_____	0._____	0._____ x 100 = _____%
10. $\frac{5}{6}$ =	_____	0._____	0._____ x 100 = _____%

Name: _____ Date: _____

Probability of an Event

Probability tells us how likely it is that something will or will not occur. When the weather forecast indicates a 30% chance of rain, it is a probability statement. Probability is usually written as a proper fraction. Probability is a **ratio** with the number of times an event occurs over the total number of times the event (possible outcomes) takes place.

Outcome is the number of possibilities that may occur in an experiment. A coin-tossing experiment has two possible outcomes. The two outcomes are the appearance of heads or tails.

The occurrence of any one of the possible outcomes (heads or tails) is an **event**. If a coin is tossed 10 times, 10 is the total number of times the event takes place. The number of times the coin lands with a head or tail showing is the **frequency** of an event.

The ratio of the frequency of heads or tails appearing in 10 tosses (outcomes) is a proper fraction, since the frequency of heads in the 10 tosses is placed over 10.

In many mathematics problems, diagrams are used to better understand the problem. In probability, diagrams can be used to help understand the outcomes. The diagram used is a **probability tree**.

Example: The outcomes in a coin-tossing experiment are illustrated by the following probability tree. If a coin is tossed one time, the probability of getting heads is $\frac{1}{2}$ and the probability of getting tails is $\frac{1}{2}$.

COIN TOSS: Probability of coin landing head or tail

1st toss	outcomes	H = head; T = Tail

$\frac{1}{2}$ head ——— H (probability = $\frac{1}{2}$)

$\frac{1}{2}$ tail ——— T (probability = $\frac{1}{2}$)

In the probability trees you will use in this section, the experiments are all probability experiments where the events are equally likely to occur. In the case of the coin toss, each time the coin is tossed, the probability remains $\frac{1}{2}$ heads and $\frac{1}{2}$ tails.

Directions: Complete the following statements.

1. In the above probability tree, the coin is tossed _____ time(s).

2. In the above probability tree, the two outcomes that may occur are _____ or

   _____.

3. The probability of getting heads is _____.

4. The probability of getting tails is _____.

5. In a coin-tossing experiment, the probability of either outcome is _____.

Name: _____ Date: _____

Probability of an Event (cont.)

In the previous probability tree, the coin was tossed one time. In the next probability tree, the coin is tossed two times. The probability that the coin will land on heads or tails on the first toss is $\frac{1}{2}$ for each. The probability that the coin will land on heads or tails on the second toss is also $\frac{1}{2}$.

PROBABILITY TREE: showing possible outcomes for a coin tossed two times

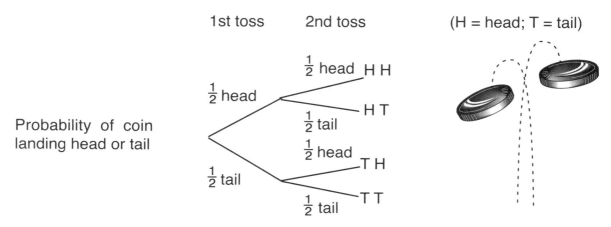

Directions: Complete the following statements.

6. In the probability tree above, the coin is tossed _____ times.

7. The two possible outcomes that may occur on each toss of the coin are _____ or

   _____.

8. Each time the coin is tossed the probability of a head or tail is the proper fraction _____.

9. In the above probability tree, the coin is tossed two times so there are _____

   outcomes.

10. The events that may occur are _____ _____, _____ _____,

    _____ _____, or _____ _____.

Directions: In the space below, develop a probability tree showing the outcomes, events, and probabilities when a coin is tossed <u>three times.</u>

Name:_____ Date: _____

 ## Probability Ratios: Between 0 and 1

It is important to point out that in determining the probability of an event, the probability ratio (proper fraction) will always be between 0 and 1. A probability of 0 means the event will never occur, while a probability of 1 means that the event will occur 100% of the time.

There are few events that occur 100% of the time or 0% of the time. The probability that the earth will be rotating tomorrow morning is 100%. The probability 100% is written as the number 1. The probability that the earth will not be rotating tomorrow morning is 0%. The probability 0% is written as 0.

The probability that any event will occur is represented between 0 and 1. Probability can be thought of in the following way. A die has six faces with the numbers 1, 2, 3, 4, 5, and 6 on them. The six numbers are all possible outcomes of the die toss. Only one of the six numbers will appear when the die is tossed. Each of the numbers is a possible outcome.

Direction: Answer the following questions.

1. If you toss the die, what is the probability that the number 7 will appear? _____

2. If you toss the die, what is the probability that one of the numbers 1, 2, 3, 4, 5, or 6 will occur?

_____

3. If you toss the die, what proper fraction represents the probability that the face with the number 1 will appear? _____

4. If you toss the die, what proper fraction represents the probability that the face with the number 5 will appear? _____

5. If you toss the die, what proper fraction represents the probability that the face with the number 6 will appear? _____

6. When a die is tossed, any one of the numbers 1, 2, 3, 4, 5, or 6 may appear on the die. In the blanks below each of the numbers, place the proper fraction that represents the probability that the number will appear when the die is tossed.

    1   2   3   4   5   6

$$\frac{}{6} + \frac{}{6} + \frac{}{6} + \frac{}{6} + \frac{}{6} + \frac{}{6} = \frac{6}{6} = \underline{}$$

7. When an outcome is certain to occur, the probability is the number _____.

8. When an outcome is certain not to occur, the probability is the number _____.

9. When the probability of an outcome is neither 1 nor 0, then the probability will be a

_____ _____ between 0 and 1.

Probability Ratios: Between 0 and 1 (cont.)

A bag has a green marble, a blue marble, a red marble, and a white marble in it. You are to draw marbles from the bag one at a time without looking.

10. The probability that you will draw a white marble the first time you draw is represented by the proper fraction _____.

11. The probability that you will draw a red marble the first time you draw is _____.

12. The probability that you will draw a blue marble the first time you draw is _____.

13. The probability that you will draw a green marble the first time you draw is _____.

14. If you draw four times, the probability that you will draw a green, red, blue, and white marble is $\overline{4} + \overline{4} + \overline{4} + \overline{4} = \overline{4} = 1$

15. If a bag has a green, red, blue, and white marble, the probability that you will draw either a green, red, blue, or white marble is the number _____.

16. If a bag has a green, red, blue, and white marble in it, the probability that you will draw a black marble is _____.

Directions: Answer the following questions about probability.

17. The probability of an event is always between _____ and _____.

18. A coin has heads on both sides. When the coin is tossed, the probability that it will land heads up is the number _____.

19. A coin has heads on both sides. When the coin is tossed, the probability that it will land tails up is the number _____.

20. A coin has a head on one side and a tail on the other side. When the coin is tossed, the probability that it will land heads up is the proper fraction _____.

21. A coin has a head on one side and a tail on the other side. When the coin is tossed, the probability that it will land tails up is the proper fraction _____.

Directions: Circle the correct answer.

22. A coin has a head on one side and a tail on the other side. When the coin is tossed, the probability that it will land either heads up or tails up is [one/zero].

23. A coin has a head on one side and a tail on the other side. When the coin is tossed, the probability that it will land neither heads up nor tails up is [one/zero].

Name:_____ Date: _____

Heads or Tails?

When probability is stated as a proper fraction, it is always between 0 and 1. When a coin is tossed, there are two **outcomes**. Each of the outcomes is an **event**. The probability that the event will result in a head or tail is $\frac{1}{2}$ for heads and $\frac{1}{2}$ for tails. So the probability of tails plus the probability of heads equals the one coin-tossing event. Therefore, $\frac{1}{2} + \frac{1}{2} = 1$.

If a coin is tossed 5 times and the coin lands heads up three times and tails up twice, the ratios are $\frac{3}{5}$ (heads) and $\frac{2}{5}$ (tails). Adding $\frac{3}{5} + \frac{2}{5} = \frac{5}{5} = 1$.

A coin is tossed 10 times. The 10 tosses are H, H, T, H, T, T, T, H, H, H. The total number of tosses is 10. The number of H's is six. The number of T's is four. The frequency of heads is six times in the 10 tosses or $\frac{6}{10}$. The frequency of tails is four times in the 10 tosses or $\frac{4}{10}$.

The coin-tossing event above took place 10 times. The event of the coin landing heads up occurred six times. The probability ratio for heads is the proper fraction $\frac{6}{10}$. The event of the coin landing tails up occurred four times. The probability ratio for tails is the proper fraction $\frac{4}{10}$. Adding the proper fractions representing the probability ratios, $\frac{6}{10} + \frac{4}{10}$, equals 1.

Directions: Answer the following questions.

1. The number of times the coin-tossing event occurred in the paragraph above is _____.

2. The frequency of a head in the ten tosses of the coin is _____.

3. The frequency of a tail in the ten tosses of the coin is _____.

4. The fraction that represents the number of heads in the ten tosses is _____.

5. The proper fraction in Question 4 changed to a proper fraction in simplified form is _____.

6. The fraction that represents the number of tails in the ten tosses is the fraction _____.

7. The proper fraction in Question 6 changed to a proper fraction in simplified form is _____.

Directions: Circle the fraction represented by the statement.

8. The coin is tossed ten times and lands tails up three of those times. $\frac{1}{10}$ $\frac{6}{10}$ $\frac{5}{10}$ $\frac{3}{10}$

9. The coin is tossed ten times and lands tails up seven of those times. $\frac{8}{10}$ $\frac{7}{10}$ $\frac{3}{10}$ $\frac{2}{10}$

10. The coin is tossed ten times and lands heads up eight of those times $\frac{8}{10}$ $\frac{4}{10}$ $\frac{9}{10}$ $\frac{6}{10}$

11. The coin is tossed five times and lands tails up two of those times. $\frac{1}{5}$ $\frac{4}{5}$ $\frac{3}{5}$ $\frac{2}{5}$

12. The coin is tossed five times and lands heads up four of those times. $\frac{2}{5}$ $\frac{3}{5}$ $\frac{4}{5}$ $\frac{1}{5}$

Name:_____ Date:_____

 # A Coin-Tossing Experiment

Directions: In the next exercise, you are to toss a coin ten times and, in each rectangle, record a head or tail after each toss. Before you begin the coin-tossing experiment, answer questions 1 and 2.

1. I predict that there will be ____ heads in the ten tosses of the coin.

2. I predict that there will be ____ tails in the ten tosses of the coin.

Now begin the coin-tossing experiment. After each toss of the coin, record the result in the chart below.

1.	2.	3.	4.	5.
6.	7.	8.	9.	10.

Directions: Answer the following questions.

3. The total number of events is _____.

4. The number of heads is _____.

5. The number of tails is _____.

6. The fraction representing the number of heads is _____.

7. The prediction I made in question 1 was that the coin would land heads up _____ of the time.

8. The fraction in question 6 changed to simplified form is _____.

9. The fraction representing the number of tails is _____.

10. The fraction in question 9 changed to simplified form is _____.

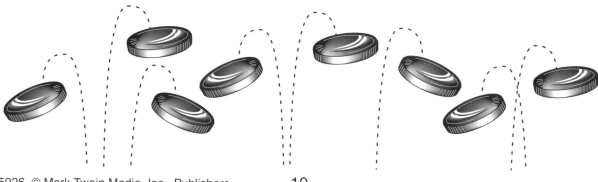

Name:_____ Date: _____

 # How Many Outcomes?

In probability, it is important to know how many different outcomes may occur. In the case of a coin toss, there are two outcomes. Each of the outcomes is either the possibility heads-up or tails-up.

Directions: Complete the statements that follow.

1. When a coin is tossed, _____ outcomes may occur.

2. Each event (toss of the coin) may result in the coin landing with a _____ or

_____ showing.

When a die is tossed, any one of the numbers 1, 2, 3, 4, 5, or 6 may appear. The die tossing is an event, and any one of the six numbers on the face of the die may appear. The probability that any one of the numbers will appear is the proper fraction $\frac{1}{6}$.

3. Each of the numbers that may appear when the die is rolled are listed below. In the blank below each of the numbers, write the proper fraction indicating the probability that the number will appear when the die is tossed.

1   2   3   4   5   6

___ + ___ + ___ + ___ + ___ + ___ = ___ = ___

Directions: In the next exercise, you will toss a die six times. After each toss, record the result in the chart below. Before beginning the experiment, answer question 4.

4. I predict that each of the numbers on the die will appear _____ time(s) in the six tosses of the die.

Begin the die-tossing experiment. In the chart below, record the number on the die that appears face-up after each toss of the die.

Toss	1	2	3	4	5	6

5. How close were your predictions to your results? Can you think of any reasons why your predictions and results might vary, even though your predictions were realistic?

_____

_____

_____

_____

Name: _____ Date: _____

 A Die-Tossing Experiment

Directions: There are 36 rectangles in the chart below. You will toss the die 36 times in this exercise. Before beginning the exercise, fill in the following blanks.

1. I predict that the number of 1's will be _____, the number of 2's will be _____, the number

of 3's _____, the number of 4's _____, the number of 5's _____, and the number of 6's

_____.

Now toss the die 36 times and record the number that appears each time in the chart below. Each of the rectangles must show the number that appears on the face of the die after each toss.

2. In the blanks below, list the number of times each of the numbers from the face of the die appears in the rectangles.

1: _____   2: _____   3: _____   4: _____   5: _____   6: _____

3. In the following exercise, place the numbers from the blanks in question 2 as the numerators over the denominator (36) to make proper fractions.

1:          2:   3:   4:   5:   6:

_____   _____   _____   _____   _____   _____
  36   36   36   36   36   36

4. In the blanks below, compare your prediction with the numbers that appeared when the die was tossed.

	1	2	3	4	5	6
Prediction:	_____	_____	_____	_____	_____	_____
Actual:	_____	_____	_____	_____	_____	_____

Name:_____ Date: _____

More Die Tossing

Directions: In the following exercise, the die is to be tossed 36 times. The number that appears on the face of the die is to be recorded in the chart below next to the numbers. Before beginning the exercise, complete the following prediction.

1. I predict that the numbers 1, 3, and 5 will appear _____ times in the 36 tosses. The proper

fraction representing the number of times a 1, 3, or 5 appears will be _____.

Simplified, the proper fraction will be _____.

2. I predict that the numbers 2, 4, and 6 will appear _____ times in the 36 tosses. The proper

fraction representing the number of times a 2, 4, or 6 will appear will be _____.

Simplified, the proper fraction will be _____.

3.

Number Appearing on Face of Die	Tally	Proper Fraction
1, 3, 5		
2, 4, 6		

Name:_____ Date: _____

Review and Practice Lesson 1

Directions: Simplify the following proper fractions. After simplifying them, write the decimal equivalent (rounded to the nearest hundredth) and then write it as a percent.

1. $\frac{2}{4}$ = _____ = _____ = _____ %

5. $\frac{8}{10}$ = _____ = _____ = _____ %

2. $\frac{3}{6}$ = _____ = _____ = _____ %

6. $\frac{3}{9}$ = _____ = _____ = _____ %

3. $\frac{4}{10}$ = _____ = _____ = _____ %

7. $\frac{6}{10}$ = _____ = _____ = _____ %

4. $\frac{8}{12}$ = _____ = _____ = _____ %

8. $\frac{4}{6}$ = _____ = _____ = _____ %

Directions: Fill in the blanks with one of the following terms. Some may be used more than once.

**probability, event, outcomes, ratio, two, six, proper,
fraction, numerator, denominator**

9. The tossing of a coin or die is called a(n) _____.

10. The ratio that expresses the number of times an event occurs is the _____ of the event.

11. In the case of tossing a coin for each event, there are _____ possible _____.

12. In the case of tossing a die for each event, there are _____ possible _____.

13. The probability of an event is always a(n) _____ fraction.

14. The proper fraction in probability is a(n) _____ between zero and one.

15. In a proper fraction, the _____ is smaller than the _____.

Directions: Determine the probability in fraction form for each of the following problems.

16. The probability that a tail will occur when a coin is tossed is _____.

17. The probability that a five will appear when a die is tossed is _____.

18. The probability that a 1, 2, 3, 4, 5, or 6 will appear when a die is tossed is _____.

19. The probability that a 7 will appear when a typical die is tossed is _____.

20. The probability that a head or tail will appear when a coin is tossed is _____.

21. When a coin with heads on one side and tails on the other is tossed, the probability that something other than a head or tail will appear is _____.

Name:_____ Date: _____

 Pick a Number: Numbers

Directions: To complete the next exercise, it will be necessary to use a pair of scissors to cut out each of the circled numbers. In cutting out the circled numbers, be careful that all are the same size.

1	2	3	4	5
6	7	8	9	10
11	12	13	14	15
16	17	18	19	20
21	22	23	24	25
26	27	28	29	30
31	32	33	34	35
36	37	38	39	40

Name:_____ Date: _____

Pick a Number

Directions: Follow the instructions and then answer the questions.

Place the circles numbered 1–10 from the previous page in a bag. Draw one circle out of the bag. Place the number drawn back in the bag before the next drawing each time.

1. The probability that a circle drawn from the bag will have the number 4 on it is represented by the proper fraction _____.

2. The probability that a circle drawn from the bag will have the number 8 on it is represented by the decimal _____.

3. The probability that a circle drawn from the bag will have the number 2 on it is represented by the percent _____.

4. The probability that any of the numbers 1–10 will be drawn from the bag is the proper fraction _____, the decimal _____, or the percent _____.

In this exercise, you will work with a partner. First place the circles numbered 1–10 in a bag. Your partner will shake the bag so that the 10 circles are mixed. Without looking, you will then draw a circle from the bag. After each draw, record the number in the chart below and replace the circle in the bag. After your friend shakes the bag, draw again. This should be continued until you have drawn 10 times. Repeat the process for your partner. Each of you should record your results on your own chart.

Beginning with the rectangle on the left, write the number drawn in a rectangle. Continue drawing until each of the 10 rectangles has a number recorded in it.

5. Do all 10 numbers (1–10) appear in the chart above? _____

6. Were any numbers (1–10) drawn and recorded more than one time? _____

Now place all 40 of the circled numbers in the bag and mix them thoroughly. Answer the following questions.

7. The probability that a circle drawn from the bag will have the number 4 on it is represented by the proper fraction _____.

Pick a Number (cont.)

8. The probability that a circle drawn from the bag will have the number 8 on it is represented by the decimal _____.

9. The probability that a circle drawn from the bag will have the number 2 on it is represented by the percent _____.

10. The probability that any of the numbers 1–40 will be drawn from the bag is the proper fraction _____, the decimal _____, or the percent _____.

Now you and your partner will alternate drawing circles and holding the bag. First place the 40 circled numbers in the bag and mix them thoroughly. After each drawing, the circled number drawn will be placed back in the bag for the next draw. Record the results of each draw in the chart below.

To answer the following questions, assume that forty red-colored rectangles were numbered with a number 1 through 40. Assume the rectangles were then placed in a bag and drawn from the bag one at a time without looking.

11. The probability of drawing a red rectangle with the number 5 on it is the proper fraction _____, the decimal _____, or the percent _____.

12. The probability of drawing a red rectangle with the number 10 on it is the proper fraction _____, the decimal _____, or the percent _____.

13. The probability of drawing a red rectangle with a number 1 through 10 on it is the proper fraction _____, the decimal _____, or the percent _____.

14. The probability of drawing a red rectangle with a number 11 through 30 on it is the proper fraction _____, the decimal _____, or the percent _____.

15. The probability of drawing a green rectangle with the number 5 on it is represented by the percent _____.

16. The probability of drawing a red rectangle with one of the numbers 1–40 on it is represented by the percent _____.

Name:_____ Date: _____

Review and Practice Lesson 2

Directions: In the next exercise, you will need a coin and pencil. You will toss the coin 20 times and record the results of each event in the chart below. After recording the 20 outcomes of tossing the coin, answer the questions that follow.

Chart 1

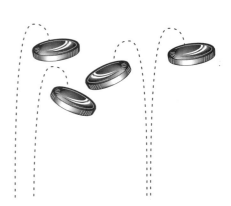

1. Each event has _____ outcomes that may occur.

2. In the twenty tosses of the coin, _____ were heads.

3. In the twenty tosses of the coin, _____ were tails.

4. Add the two proper fractions in questions 3 and 4.

$$\frac{}{20} + \frac{}{20} = \frac{}{} = \_\_\_\_$$

The results of experiments like the 20 tosses of the coin are used to make predictions about similar future experiments. However, sometimes an experiment is so small that the results cannot be used to make predictions with confidence.

Directions: In the next exercise, you will need a coin and pencil. Toss the coin 100 times and record the results in the chart on the next page. Answer the next two questions before beginning the 100 tosses of the coin.

5. Based on the results of the 20 tosses of the coin, I predict that there will be _____ heads in the 100 tosses. The prediction as a proper fraction is _____. In simplified form, the proper fraction is _____, the decimal _____, or the percent _____.

6. Based on the results of the 20 tosses of the coin, I predict that there will be _____ tails in the 100 tosses. The prediction as a proper fraction is _____. In simplified form, the proper fraction is _____, the decimal _____, or the percent _____.

Name:_____ Date:_____

 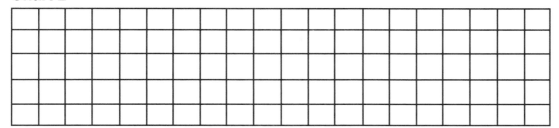 **Review and Practice Lesson 2 (cont.)**

Record the results of the 100 tosses in the chart below. After completing the 100 tosses, answer the questions that follow.

Chart 2

7. Each of the tosses of the coin is an _____.

8. When the coin is tossed, it is equally likely that the outcome will be _____

or _____.

9. In the 100 tosses of the coin, a head appeared _____ times. That is written as the proper

fraction _____, the decimal _____, or the percent _____.

10. In the 100 tosses of the coin, a tail appeared _____ times. That is written as the proper

fraction _____, the decimal _____, or the percent _____.

Directions: In an experiment, the results of one experiment are compared to the results of another experiment. Often the experiments are the same except for one thing that is different. In answering the following questions, use the information found in Charts 1 and 2.

11. In the two coin-tossing experiments, the only difference is in the _____ of

tosses of the coin.

12. In Chart 1, _____% of the tosses were heads and _____% of the tosses were tails.

13. In Chart 2, _____% of the tosses were heads and _____% of the tosses were tails.

14. The difference in percent of heads between Charts 1 and 2 is _____%.

15. The difference in percent of tails between Charts 1 and 2 is _____%.

Name:_____ Date: _____

Review and Practice Lesson 2 (cont.)

In an experiment that has been performed a number of times, there is an expected probability that a specific event will occur. In the case of tossing a coin, the expected probability that the outcome will be a head or tail is $\frac{1}{2}$ heads and $\frac{1}{2}$ tails.

16. In the coin-tossing experiments, I expected the results in Chart _____ to be closest to the expected outcome of $\frac{1}{2}$ heads and $\frac{1}{2}$ tails.

17. In the actual results of the coin-tossing experiments recorded in Charts 1 and 2, I found the results in Chart _____ were closest to the expected outcome of $\frac{1}{2}$ heads and $\frac{1}{2}$ tails.

In an experiment, increasing the times an event might occur increases the number of outcomes. This, in turn, increases the confidence one can have in using the results to predict the probability that future experiments will produce a specific result.

18. In the case of the coin-tossing experiments recorded in Charts 1 and 2, I would expect the results in Chart _____ to be most accurate for making future coin-tossing predictions.

19. In predicting the probability of the event heads or tails, the results of which of the following experiments are likely to be most accurate? _____

A. The coin is tossed 10 times and the results are recorded.

B. The coin is tossed 1,000 times and the results are recorded.

C. The coin is tossed 100 times and the results are recorded.

D. The coin is tossed 50 times and the results are recorded.

20. Increasing the number of _____ of an experiment increases the _____ one can have in making _____.

Name:_____ Date: _____

Population Sampling

In the probability problems that follow, it is important to know the terms *population, sample,* and *random selection.*

Population in probability is the term used to refer to the entire group of interest. If there is interest in predicting what the free-throwing ability of the 25 players on the basketball squad might be, then the 25 players are the population.

Sample in probability is the term used to refer to a part of the entire group of interest. If five members of the 25-member squad of basketball players are selected to determine how well the squad shoots free throws, the five members are a sample of the population.

Random selection means that every member of a group is equally likely to be selected to be part of a sample.

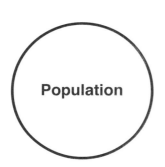 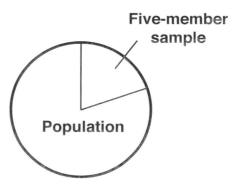

The data gathered from the sample is used to make inferences about the population. An **inference** is a conclusion arrived at from the evidence available and can be useful even though all members of the population were not used in gathering the data. The sample size is very important in determining how much confidence one can have when making an inference that what one finds is true for the sample is also true for the population.

The coach of the 25-member basketball squad wants to improve the free-throw-shooting skill of the squad. The coach decides to use a new free-throw-shooting technique. However, the coach does not have time to teach the method to all 25 members of the squad. He decides to select a sample of five squad members and teach the technique to the sample members. The coach will compare the free-throw shooting of the five-member sample group with the free-throwing shooting of the 25 squad members. If the five-member sample group's free-throw shooting is better than the free-throw shooting of the 25 squad members, the coach will infer that the new free-throw-shooting technique is better and teach it to all 25 squad members.

In selecting the sample group of five team members from the 25 member squad, the coach wants to randomly select the five-member sample group. Random selection means that every member of the squad will have an equal chance of being selected for the five-member sample group.

Name:_____ Date: _____

Population Sampling (cont.)

Directions: Complete the following.

1. *Population* refers to _____

_____

2. *Sample* refers to _____

_____

3. *Random selection* means _____

_____

4. The five-member free-throwing group is an example of a _____.

5. The 25-member basketball squad is an example of a _____.

6. If all members of a population have an equal chance of being selected for a sample group,

then there has been a _____ selection.

The coach knows that if the selection of the five-member sample group is random, then each member of the 25-member squad must have an equal opportunity of being selected for the sample group. The coach decides to use the procedure below to make sure that there is a random selection.

Step 1: Each member of the 25-member basketball squad will be assigned a number.

Step 2: Each of the numbers will be written on pieces of paper that are identical in size, shape, and texture.

Step 3: The pieces of paper will then be placed in a paper sack.

Step 4: The sack will be shaken so that the 25 pieces of paper are thoroughly mixed.

Step 5: Without looking in the sack, five pieces of paper will be drawn from the sack one at a time.

Step 6: The five members of the basketball squad whose numbers were drawn become the sample group to be taught the new free-throwing technique.

Population Sampling (cont.)

The five members of the sample group were taught the new free-throwing technique. The chart below shows the free-throwing results of the five-member sample group after the free-throwing technique had been taught to each of them.

Percent Free Throws Made

Member B 60%	Member E 80%	Member J 50%	Member O 70%	Member W 90%

The chart below is the free-throwing results for all 25 members of the basketball squad without using the new free-throwing technique. Compare the results of the two charts and determine if the coach should teach the new free-throwing technique to the team.

Percent Free Throws Made

Member A 60%	Member B 50%	Member C 40%	Member D 30%	Member E 65%
Member F 70%	Member G 55%	Member H 65%	Member I 30%	Member J 50%
Member K 80%	Member L 50%	Member M 68%	Member N 73%	Member O 60%
Member P 50%	Member Q 62%	Member R 70%	Member S 45%	Member T 80%
Member U 20%	Member V 70%	Member W 70%	Member X 40%	Member Y 55%

7. Should the coach teach the free-throwing technique to all 25 members of the squad?

_____

Name: _____ Date: _____

Sample Space

You have learned some very important vocabulary words associated with probability experiments, words like *population, sample, outcome, event, random selection,* and *prediction.*

Another important term to know is the term *sample space.* **Sample space** is all of the possible outcomes. The sample space for the random selection of the sample of five free-throwers is the 25-member basketball squad. Any one of the 25 members of the basketball squad has an equal chance of being selected as a member of the sample of five free-throwers.

Directions: The following questions are to help you understand the term *sample space.* When answering each question, remember that a sample space is all of the possible outcomes that may occur.

1. When a coin is tossed, the sample space is that the coin may land with a _____ or

_____ showing.

2. When a die is tossed, the sample space is the numbers ____ , 2, ____, ____, ____, and ____.

3. When a pair of dice are tossed, the sample space is the numbers ____, ____, ____, ____,

____, ____, ____, 8, ____, ____, 11, and ____.

4. The numbers 10, 20, 30, 40, 50, 60, and 70 are written on small pieces of paper and placed

in a bag. All of the numbers have an equal opportunity of being drawn. The sample space

is the numbers _____, _____, _____, _____, _____, _____, and _____.

5. Twenty marbles are placed in a bag. Ten of the marbles are green, five are black, and five

are red. All of the marbles have an equal opportunity of being drawn from the bag. The

sample space is _____ marbles.

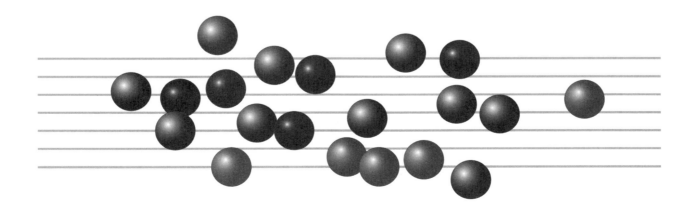

Name:_____ Date: _____

 ## Sample Space (cont.)

Three marbles are placed in a bag. One marble is red, one is green, and one is black.

6. The probability that a red marble will be drawn is the proper fraction _____, the decimal

_____, or the percent _____.

7. The probability that a black marble will be drawn is the proper fraction _____, the decimal

_____, or the percent _____.

8. The probability that a green marble will be drawn is the proper fraction _____, the decimal

_____, or the percent _____.

9. The probability that a white marble will be drawn is _____%.

10. The probability that a red, green, or black marble will be drawn is _____%.

The names of 100 persons are written on pieces of paper and placed in a box. Each piece of paper has a different name written on it. The pieces of paper each have an equal chance of being drawn from the box. Answer the following questions using the terms **random sample**, **sample space**, **population**, and **sample**.

11. The 100 persons are known as the _____.

12. It is decided that 10 of the names will be drawn from the box. The 10 names drawn are called

a _____.

13. Each of the 100 names in the box has an equal chance of being one of the ten names drawn.

The ten names drawn are an example of a _____ _____.

14. Since any one of the 100 names may be a possible outcome, the 100 names are the

_____ _____.

Name:_____ Date: _____

Sampling Practice: Numbers

The following numbers are the weights of 25 different breeds of full-grown dogs. When full grown, some of the dogs are very large and some are very small.

Weights of 25 different dogs in pounds

10	20	30	40	50
60	70	80	90	100
110	120	130	140	150
160	170	180	190	200
210	220	230	240	250

Directions: The next exercise is designed to give you more practice in using the sampling technique. Cut out each of the rectangles with the weight of a breed of dog.

Name:_____ Date: _____

Sampling Practice

Step 1: Place the 25 rectangles in a bag and shake thoroughly. Then, without looking in the bag, draw five rectangles from the bag one at a time.

Step 2: Record the weights on the five rectangles drawn in the chart below.

Chart 1

Step 3: Find the sum of the five weights in the chart. _____

Step 4: Divide the sum in Step 3 by five to find the average weight of the five-dog sample.

_____

Directions: Answer the following questions. Circle the correct answers where appropriate.

1. The 25 weights are a [population/sample].

2. The five weights selected from the bag are a [population/sample].

3. Since all 25 dog weights have an equal opportunity to be drawn, the sample is

_____.

4. Since each of the dog weights had an equal chance of being drawn, there are _____ members of the sample space.

5. In this experiment, there are _____ possible outcomes.

6. The average weight of the five-dog sample recorded in the chart is _____ pounds.

7. Based on the average weight of the five dogs, I predict that the average weight of the 25 dogs is _____ pounds.

Directions: For the next exercise, place the 25 rectangles with the dog weights in the bag again. Shake the bag to thoroughly mix the rectangles. Repeat the sampling procedure, this time drawing ten rectangles. Record the ten weights in Chart 2.

Chart 2

Step 5: Find the sum of the ten weights in Chart 2, and divide by 10 to find the average weight of the ten-dog sample.

8. The average weight of the ten-dog sample recorded in Chart 2 is _____ pounds.

9. Based on the average found in Question 8, I predict the average weight of the 25 dogs is

_____ pounds.

Name:_____ Date: _____

Sampling Practice (cont.)

Directions: Place the 25 rectangles back in the bag. Shake the bag to thoroughly mix the rectangles. Repeat the sampling procedure, this time drawing 20 rectangles. Record the 20 weights in Chart 3.

Chart 3

Step 6: Find the sum of the weights recorded on the 20 rectangles, and divide the sum by 20 to find the average weight of the sample.

10. The average weight in the 20-dog sample in Chart 3 is _____ pounds.

11. The sample size in Chart 1 is **A)** _____, in Chart 2 is **B)** _____, and in Chart 3 is **C)** _____.

Step 7: Find the sum of the weights of the population of 25 dogs. Divide the sum by 25 to find the actual average weight of the population.

12. The average weight of the population of 25 dogs is _____ pounds.

13. The sample closest to the actual average weight of the population of 25 dogs is the sample in Chart _____.

14. It is expected that the larger the _____, the greater the confidence that accurate predictions can be made about the population from which the sample is drawn.

Name: _____ Date: _____

Probability When Outcomes Are Not Equally Likely

In studying probability problems where a fair coin or die is tossed, each of the outcomes is equally likely to occur. When a coin is tossed, the likelihood of a tail is the same as the likelihood of a head. The probability of each is $\frac{1}{2}$. In the case of a die, the likelihood of one of the numbers 1, 2, 3, 4, 5, or 6 appearing is equally likely. The probability of any one of the numbers appearing when the die is tossed is $\frac{1}{6}$.

In many probability problems, however, all outcomes are not equally likely. The probability of the outcomes cannot be represented by the same proper fraction. The next exercise will help you understand outcomes that are not equally likely.

Directions: Answer the following questions about each situation.

Five marbles are placed in a bag. The five marbles are all black. There are no other objects in the bag.

1. If one marble is drawn from the bag, the marble is what fraction of the five marbles? _____

2. The fraction representing the four marbles remaining in the bag is _____.

3. The probability that a black marble will be drawn from the bag is _____ or _____%.

4. The probability that a white marble will be drawn from the bag is _____ or _____%.

Five marbles are placed in a bag. One marble is white, one marble is red, and three marbles are black.

5. The proper fraction representing one of the five marbles is _____.

6. The proper fraction representing the three black marbles is _____.

7. The proper fraction representing the white marble is _____.

8. The proper fraction representing the red marble is _____.

9. Place the fractions in Questions 6, 7, and 8 in the blanks below and find the sum.

_____ + _____ + _____ = _____

Name:_____ Date: _____

Probability When Outcomes Are Not Equally Likely (cont.)

The three black marbles, one white marble, and one red marble are placed in the bag and drawn one at a time. After each marble is drawn, it is placed back in the bag before the next draw takes place.

10. There are _____ possible outcomes in this experiment.

11. Each of the outcomes is an _____.

12. The probability that a white marble will be drawn is the proper fraction _____.

13. The probability that a black marble will be drawn is the proper fraction _____.

14. The probability that a red marble will be drawn is the proper fraction _____.

Twelve marbles are placed in a bag. One of the marbles is white, two marbles are green, three marbles are red, and six marbles are blue. The marbles will be drawn one at a time. After each draw, the marble drawn will be placed back in the bag.

15. There are _____ possible outcomes in this experiment.

16. Each of the outcomes is an _____.

17. The probability that a white marble will be drawn is the proper fraction _____, which in simplified form is _____, the decimal _____, or _____%.

18. The probability that a red marble will be drawn is the proper fraction _____, which in simplified form is _____, the decimal _____, or _____%.

19. The probability that a blue marble will be drawn is the proper fraction _____, which in simplified form is _____, the decimal _____, or _____%.

20. The probability that a green marble will be drawn from the bag is the proper fraction _____, which in simplified form is _____, the decimal _____, or _____%.

21. In the blanks below, place the answers given for the percents in Questions 17, 18, 19, and 20.

_____% + _____% + _____% + _____% = _____%

Name:_____ Date: _____

Probability: Going Around in Circles

Directions: In answering the following questions, refer to Circle A, Circle B, and Circle C below. In each question, the arrow has been spun and will not be interfered with until it stops.

A.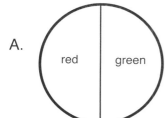

B.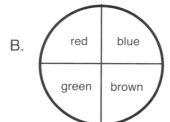

C.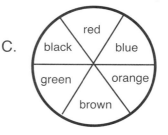

1. In Circle A, the probability that the spinning arrow will stop on green is _____.

2. In Circle B, the probability that the spinning arrow will stop on blue is _____.

3. In Circle C, the probability that the spinning arrow will stop on red is _____.

4. In Circle C, the probability that the spinning arrow will stop on blue is _____.

5. In Circle C, the probability that the spinning arrow will stop on red or blue is _____.

6. In Circle C, the probability that the spinning arrow will stop on green is _____.

Directions: In answering the following questions, refer to Circle D, Circle E, and Circle F.

D.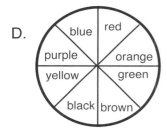

E.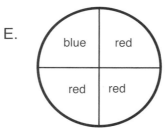

F.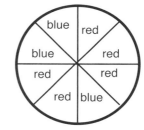

7. In Circle D, the probability that the spinning arrow will stop on red is:
   A) $\frac{1}{2}$ **B)** $\frac{1}{4}$ **C)** $\frac{3}{4}$ **D)** $\frac{1}{8}$

8. In Circle D, the probability that the spinning arrow will stop on blue is:
   A) $\frac{1}{2}$ **B)** $\frac{1}{4}$ **C)** $\frac{3}{4}$ **D)** $\frac{1}{8}$

9. In Circle E, the probability that the spinning arrow will stop on red is:
   A) $\frac{1}{2}$ **B)** $\frac{1}{4}$ **C)** $\frac{3}{4}$ **D)** $\frac{1}{8}$

10. In Circle E, the probability that the spinning arrow will stop on blue is:
    A) $\frac{1}{2}$ **B)** $\frac{1}{4}$ **C)** $\frac{3}{4}$ **D)** $\frac{1}{8}$

11. In Circle F, the probability that the spinning arrow will stop on red is:
    A) $\frac{5}{8}$ **B)** $\frac{1}{8}$ **C)** $\frac{3}{8}$ **D)** $\frac{7}{8}$

12. In Circle F, the probability that the spinning arrow will stop on blue is:
    A) $\frac{5}{8}$ **B)** $\frac{1}{8}$ **C)** $\frac{3}{8}$ **D)** $\frac{7}{8}$

Name:_____ Date: _____

Review and Practice Lesson 3

The following letters are cut out and placed in a bag. The bag is shaken so that the letters are mixed. After each draw, the letter drawn is placed back in the bag.

```
E         R         R         S
H         E         H         T
S         S         F         E
R         A         R         T
S         H         T         R
```

1. There are _____ possible outcomes.

2. The letter drawn from the bag is called a(n) _____.

3. The probability that the letter R will be drawn is the proper fraction _____, simplified _____.

4. The probability that the letter R will be drawn is the decimal _____.

5. The probability that the letter R will be drawn is _____ percent.

6. The probability that the letter S will be drawn is the proper fraction _____, simplified _____.

7. The probability that the letter S will be drawn is the decimal _____.

8. The probability that the letter S will be drawn is _____ percent.

9. The probability that the letter F will be drawn is the proper fraction _____, simplified _____.

10. The probability that the letter F will be drawn is the decimal _____.

11. The probability that the letter F will be drawn is _____ percent.

12. The probability that any of the letters will be drawn is a proper fraction between _____

    and _____.

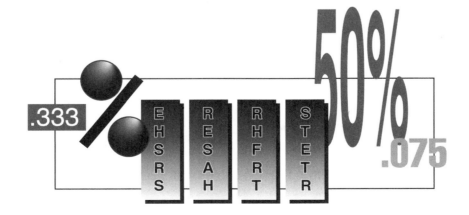

Name:_____ Date: _____

 Understanding Mutually Exclusive Events

In solving probability problems, knowing when an event is **mutually exclusive** is very important. An event is mutually exclusive when only one outcome can happen at a time. An example of a mutually exclusive event is the tossing of a die. When the die is tossed, it can land with only one number showing. The number showing is a mutually exclusive outcome.

You will often find probability problems asking you to find the probability that any **set** of mutually exclusive outcomes will occur. For example, what is the probability that when a die is tossed a one **or** three will occur?

The rule for finding the probability that a set of mutually exclusive outcomes will occur is the **addition rule**. The addition rule states that the probability of the mutually occurring outcomes is the sum of the probabilities of each event.

Example: What is the probability that a one or three will appear when a die is tossed? The probability that a one will occur when the die is tossed is one-sixth. The probability that a three will occur is also one-sixth.

Addition rule: $\frac{1}{6} + \frac{1}{6} = \frac{2}{6} = \frac{1}{3}$

The probability that the mutually exclusive outcome of a one showing on the die or the mutually exclusive outcome of a three showing on the die is one-third.

1. The probability that a two or four will appear when a die is tossed is ____.

2. The probability that a five or six will appear when a die is tossed is ____ .

3. The probability that a three or four or five will appear when a die is tossed is ____ or _____%.

4. The probability that a two or three or four or six will appear when a die is tossed is ____ or _____%.

5. The even numbers that are on the die are ____, ____, and ____.

6. The probability that an even number will appear when a die is tossed is ____ or _____%.

7. The odd numbers that are on the die are ____, ____, and ____.

8. The probability that an odd number will appear when a die is tossed is ____ or _____%.

9. The probability that a one or two or three or four or five or six will appear when a die is tossed is ____ or _____%.

10. The probability that a zero or seven will appear when a typical die is tossed is ____ or _____%.

Name:_____ Date: _____

More Mutually Exclusive Events

Directions: Complete the following exercises.

A green, red, black, and white marble are placed in a bag.

1. The probability that a green or black marble will be drawn from the bag is ___ or _____%.

2. The probability that a black or white marble will be drawn from the bag is ___ or _____%.

3. The probability that a green or red or white marble will be drawn is ___ or _____%.

4. The probability is $\frac{4}{4}$ or 1 that a _____ or _____ or _____ or

_____ marble will be drawn.

5. The probability that a tossed coin will land heads or tails is ___ + ___ = ___ = ___.

In an eighth grade class, there are 25 students. Ten have black hair, five have red hair, and ten have blond hair. Solve the following problems:

6. The probability that the first student who comes into the classroom will have black hair is

_____%.

7. The probability that the first student who comes into the classroom will have red hair is

_____%.

8. The probability that the first student who comes into the classroom will have blond hair is

_____%.

9. The probability that the first student who comes into the classroom will have black hair or

red hair is _____%.

10. The probability that the first student who comes into the classroom will have black hair or

blond hair is _____%.

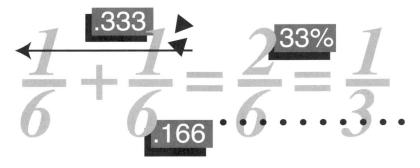

Name:_____ Date: _____

 ## Independent Events

A die is tossed two times. What is the probability that a one and three will appear? Note that in this problem, the probability question is specific to the appearance of a one on the first toss followed by a three on the second toss. The one and three are each **independent events**. Events are independent when the occurrence of one does not influence the occurrence of the other.

To solve this type of problem, the probability of the independent events are multiplied. The probability of the one appearing when a die is tossed is one-sixth. The probability of the three appearing when a die is tossed is one-sixth. To solve the problem, the probabilities are multiplied.

$$\frac{1}{6} \text{ times } \frac{1}{6} = \frac{1}{36} \text{ or } 0.0277 \text{ or } 3\%$$

1. The probability that when a die is tossed a two will appear on the first toss and a six on the second toss is ___ x ___ = ___ = _____%.

2. The probability that when a die is tossed a three will appear on the first toss and a four on the second toss is ___ x ___ = ___ = _____%.

3. The probability that when a die is tossed a two will appear on the first toss, a two on the second toss, and a five on the third toss is ___ x ___ x ___ = ___ = _____%.

4. The probability that a tossed coin will land heads on the first toss and heads on the second toss is ___ x ___ = ___ = _____%.

5. The probability that a tossed coin will land heads on the first toss and tails on the second toss is ___ x ___ = ___ = _____%.

6. The probability that a tossed coin will land heads on the first toss, heads on the second toss, and tails on the third toss is ___ x ___ x ___ = ___ = _____%.

7. The probability that a tossed coin will land heads on the first toss, tails on the second toss, heads on the third toss, and tails on the fourth toss is ___ x ___ x ___ x ___ = ___ = _____%.

A bag contains four marbles, one each of the colors black, red, white, and green. The marbles are drawn from the bag one at a time.

8. The probability that the white marble will be drawn first and the red marble will be picked on the second draw is ___ or _____%.

9. The probability that the black marble will be drawn on the first draw and the white marble will be picked on the second draw is ___ or _____%.

10. The probability that the marbles will be drawn in order green, red, and white is ___ or _____%.

Name:_____ Date: _____

Review and Practice Lesson 4

In this exercise, there are seven statements. Read each of the statements and then fill in the chart. For each of the statements, indicate the experiment, number of events, possible outcomes, and probability of the outcomes.

1. A nickel is tossed 10 times and the results are recorded.

2. A die is tossed 20 times and the results are recorded.

3. Six marbles are placed in a bag and drawn one at a time. The marbles are replaced in the bag after each draw. The marbles are blue, red, black, green, white, and orange.

4. Marbles are placed in a bag and drawn one at a time. The marbles are replaced after each draw. The marbles are one blue, two red, three black, three green, five white, and six orange.

5. The arrow on Circle A is spun once.

6. The arrow on Circle B is spun once.

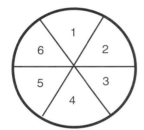 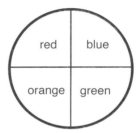

7. The arrow on Circle C is spun once.

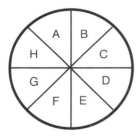

	EXPERIMENT	NUMBER OF EVENTS	OUTCOME(S)	PROBABILITY OF THE OUTCOME(S)
1.				
2.				
3.				
4.				
5.				
6.				
7.				

Name:_____ Date: _____

 ## Dependent and Independent Events

In all of the probability problems studied so far, the events were independent. Events are independent when one event does not affect the outcome of the next event.

In many probability problems, however, the outcome of one event does affect the outcome of other events. The following exercise will be used to help you better understand dependent and independent events.

Directions: In this exercise, there are two bags, labeled Bag A and Bag B, each containing five marbles. Each bag has three red and two white marbles. In the exercise, the marbles will be drawn from the bags one marble at a time. The marble drawn from Bag A **will be replaced** after each draw. The marble from Bag B **will not be replaced** after each draw.

1. The first marble is drawn from Bag A. The probability that a red marble will be drawn is:

   A) $\frac{1}{5}$ **B)** $\frac{3}{5}$ **C)** $\frac{2}{5}$ **D)** $\frac{2}{3}$

2. The first marble is drawn from Bag B. The probability that a red marble will be drawn is:

   A) $\frac{1}{5}$ **B)** $\frac{3}{5}$ **C)** $\frac{2}{5}$ **D)** $\frac{2}{3}$

3. For the second draw, Bag A will have:

   A) 2 marbles   **B)** 4 marbles   **C)** 5 marbles   **D)** 1 marble

4. For the second draw, Bag B will have:

   A) 2 marbles   **B)** 4 marbles   **C)** 5 marbles   **D)** 1 marble

Directions: In answering the following questions, it is important to know that a red marble was drawn from both bags in the first draw.

5. For the second draw, the probability that a red marble will be drawn from Bag A is:

   A) $\frac{3}{5}$ **B)** $\frac{1}{5}$ **C)** $\frac{2}{5}$ **D)** $\frac{3}{8}$

6. For the second draw, the probability that a white marble will be drawn from Bag A is:

   A) $\frac{3}{8}$ **B)** $\frac{3}{5}$ **C)** $\frac{2}{5}$ **D)** $\frac{1}{5}$

7. For the second draw, the probability that a red marble will be drawn from Bag B is:

   A) $\frac{2}{5}$ **B)** $\frac{1}{4}$ **C)** $\frac{3}{4}$ **D)** $\frac{2}{4}$

8. For the second draw, the probability that a white marble will be drawn from Bag B is:

   A) $\frac{3}{4}$ **B)** $\frac{1}{4}$ **C)** $\frac{2}{4}$ **D)** $\frac{2}{5}$

Directions: In answering the following questions, it is important to know that on the second draw, a red marble was drawn from Bag A and a white marble was drawn from Bag B.

9. For the third draw, the probability that a red marble will be drawn from Bag A is:

   A) $\frac{2}{5}$ **B)** $\frac{3}{5}$ **C)** $\frac{1}{5}$ **D)** $\frac{3}{8}$

10. For the third draw, the probability that a white marble will be drawn from Bag A is:

    A) $\frac{1}{5}$ **B)** $\frac{3}{8}$ **C)** $\frac{2}{5}$ **D)** $\frac{3}{5}$

11. For the third draw, the probability that a red marble will be drawn from Bag B is:

    A) $\frac{1}{3}$ **B)** $\frac{2}{3}$ **C)** $\frac{1}{2}$ **D)** $\frac{1}{4}$

Dependent and Independent Events (cont.)

12. For the third draw, the probability that a white marble will be drawn from Bag B is:

A) $\frac{1}{3}$ **B)** $\frac{2}{3}$ **C)** $\frac{1}{2}$ **D)** $\frac{1}{4}$

Directions: In answering the following questions, it is important to know that on the third draw, a white marble was drawn from both bags.

13. For the fourth draw, the probability that a red marble will be drawn from Bag A is:

A) $\frac{2}{5}$ **B)** $\frac{1}{5}$ **C)** $\frac{3}{5}$ **D)** $\frac{3}{8}$

14. For the fourth draw, the probability that a white marble will be drawn from Bag A is:

A) $\frac{3}{5}$ **B)** $\frac{3}{8}$ **C)** $\frac{2}{5}$ **D)** $\frac{1}{5}$

15. For the fourth draw, the probability that a red marble will be drawn from Bag B is:

A) $\frac{1}{2}$ **B)** $\frac{1}{4}$ **C)** 0   **D)** 1

16. For the fourth draw, the probability that a white marble will be drawn from Bag B is:

A) $\frac{1}{2}$ **B)** 0   **C)** $\frac{1}{4}$ **D)** 1

Directions: In answering the following questions, it is important to know that on the fourth draw, a white marble was drawn from Bag A and a red marble was drawn from Bag B.

17. For the fifth draw, the probability that a red marble will be drawn from Bag A is:

A) $\frac{2}{5}$ **B)** $\frac{3}{5}$ **C)** $\frac{1}{5}$ **D)** $\frac{3}{8}$

18. For the fifth draw, the probability that a white marble will be drawn from Bag A is:

A) $\frac{2}{5}$ **B)** $\frac{1}{5}$ **C)** $\frac{3}{5}$ **D)** $\frac{3}{8}$

19. For the fifth draw, the probability that a red marble will be drawn from Bag B is:

A) 0   **B)** 1   **C)** $\frac{1}{2}$ **D)** $\frac{1}{4}$

20. For the fifth draw, the probability that a white marble will be drawn from Bag B is:

A) $\frac{1}{2}$ **B)** 0   **C)** 1   **D)** $\frac{1}{4}$

21. After five draws there are   **A)** 4   **B)** 3   **C)** 5   **D)** 0   marbles in Bag A.

22. After five draws there are   **A)** 4   **B)** 3   **C)** 5   **D)** 0   marbles in Bag B.

23. For which bag did the probability of the color of marble that might be drawn remain the same for each draw? Bag _____

24. For which bag did the probability of the color of marble that might be drawn change after each marble was drawn? Bag _____

25. For which bag was the probability of the next draw **not dependent** on the colors of the marbles already drawn? Bag _____

26. For which bag was the probability of the next draw **dependent** on the color of marbles already drawn? Bag _____

Name:_____ Date: _____

Revisiting Probability Trees

In the next exercise, we will again visit probability trees. Remember, probability trees are diagrams often used to determine the number of outcomes in an experiment.

Directions: The probability tree at right is for a marble-drawing experiment. Each time, the marble drawn was replaced in the bag. There are three red marbles and two white marbles in the bag for the first draw. The first marble drawn was red. The second marble drawn was white.

R = Red; W = White

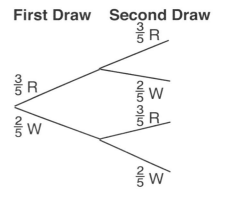

1. The probability tree shows there will be _____ draws from the bag.

2. The probability of drawing a red marble on the first draw will be _____.

3. The probability of drawing a red marble on the second draw will be _____.

4. If a third draw is made, the probability of drawing a red marble will be _____.

5. The probability of drawing a white marble on the first draw will be _____.

6. The probability of drawing a white marble on the second draw will be _____.

7. If a third draw is made, the probability of drawing a white marble will be _____.

8. The color of marble drawn on any of the draws [did/did not] affect the probability of the color of marble drawn on the next draw.

Directions: The probability tree at right is for a marble-drawing experiment where the marble drawn is not replaced in the bag. There are three red marbles and two white marbles in the bag for the first draw. The first marble drawn was red. The second marble drawn was white.

R = Red; W = White; $\frac{2}{4} = \frac{1}{2}$

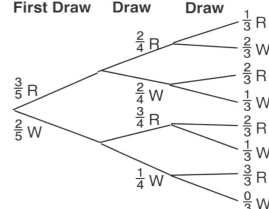

9. The probability tree shows that there will be _____ draws from the bag.

10. The probability of drawing a red marble on the third draw will be _____.

11. The probability of drawing a white marble on the second draw will be _____.

12. The color of marble drawn on any of the draws [did/did not] affect the probability of the color of marble drawn on the next draw.

Name:_____ Date: _____

 Learning More About Probability Trees

Directions: In this exercise, you will determine the possible outcomes when a die is tossed and then one of the letters A, B, or C is drawn.

1. Complete the probability tree and answer the questions that follow. Do not attempt to answer the questions until your teacher has checked the completed probability tree.

The outcomes for the toss of the die followed by the drawing of the letter are identified as 1A, 1B, and so on.

2. Complete the folowing list of outcomes:

1A, 1B, ___; ___, ___, 2C; ___, ___, ___;

___, 4B, ___; ___, ___, ___; 6A, ___, ___.

3. When the die is tossed, followed by drawing one of the three letters, _____ outcomes might occur.

4. The probability of the number 2 appearing when the die is tossed is _____.

5. The probability of the letter "C" being drawn is _____.

6. The probability that the number 3 or 4 will appear when the die is tossed is _____.

7. The probability that the letter "B" or "C" will be drawn is _____.

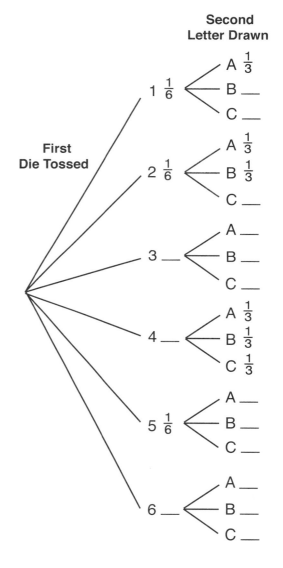

Review and Practice Lesson 5: Crossword Puzzle

Directions: Use the clues below to complete the crossword puzzle.

ACROSS

1. When a sample from the population in the probability experiment is chosen completely by chance, the sample is _____.
6. Name given to that part of the population chosen for the probability experiment (two words)
9. Number that indicates the probability that an event will absolutely occur
11. Refers to the possible events that may occur in a probability experiment
12. Diagram used to show the outcomes of a probability experiment (two words)
13. Number indicating the number of outcomes that may occur when a die is tossed
14. Number that indicates the probability that an event will absolutely not occur
15. Refers to the entire group of objects, persons, etc. that are being measured

DOWN

2. When only one event can happen at a time, the events are called _____ _____.
3. Refers to a number between zero and one that indicates the likelihood that an event will or will not occur
4. When the occurrence of one event does not influence the occurrence of the other (two words)
5. A small group of items chosen from the population in a probability experiment
7. A fraction between zero and one with the numerator smaller than the denominator (two words)
8. One of the possible outcomes of a probability experiment
10. Number indicating the number of outcomes that may occur when a coin is tossed

Name:_____ Date: _____

 ## Helping Emily Solve Problems

1. Sarah and Emily are conducting a coin-tossing experiment. The coin has been tossed ten times. The results of the ten tosses are H, H, H, H, H, H, H, H, H, H. Sarah said that because the ten tosses have all resulted in heads, the probability that the eleventh toss would be tails is greater than $\frac{1}{2}$. Emily said that she thought the probability of a tail on the eleventh toss was still $\frac{1}{2}$. Is Sarah or Emily right? Defend your answer in the space below.

_____

_____

_____

_____

_____

2. Emily read that when a die is tossed, the probability of any of the numbers 1, 2, 3, 4, 5, or 6 appearing is $\frac{1}{6}$. Emily conducted a die-tossing experiment to see if what she read was correct. After six tosses, the results are 6, 4, 4, 5, 6, 6. Emily decided that since she had tossed the die six times, each of the numbers should have appeared one time. She said that she had proven that what she had read was incorrect. Explain to Emily what is wrong with her thinking. Design an experiment that will help Emily understand why what she has read is correct.

_____

_____

_____

_____

_____

_____

Name:_____ Date: _____

Helping Emily Solve Problems (cont.)

3. Emily did an experiment with a bag that contained 25 marbles. One of the marbles was black, five were white, four were red, and the rest were green. She drew the marbles from the bag one at a time. The marble drawn was not placed back in the bag. Emily made a chart so that after each draw she would know the probability of drawing a certain color next.

The following is the order of the first ten marbles drawn:
green, green, green, white, red, green, white, white, red, green

Fill in Emily's chart.

Probability of Drawing Color

Color drawn	Green	White	Red	Black
1. green				
2. green				
3. green				
4. white				
5. red				
6. green				
7. white				
8. white				
9. red				
10. green				

4. Emily was working on probability that involved two events. She knew that to find the probability that a 1 or 4 would appear when a die was tossed, she must add the probability of the two events. Each probability is $\frac{1}{6}$, so Emily added $\frac{1}{6} + \frac{1}{6} = \frac{2}{6}$, or $\frac{1}{3}$, or 33%.

She also knew that to find the probability of a head and tail appearing when a coin was tossed, she must multiply the probabilities of each event. Each probability is $\frac{1}{2}$ so Emily multiplied $\frac{1}{2} \times \frac{1}{2} = \frac{1}{4}$, or 25%.

Emily wanted to make a probability experiment using the die and coin. She was going to toss a die and then toss the coin. Emily wanted to know the probability of a 1 on the die or a head on the coin. She knew that the "or" in the problem was a signal that she must add. Show Emily how to find the probability that a 1 on the die or a head on the coin will appear.

_____

_____

_____

Helping Emily Solve Problems (cont.)

5. Emily was again going to toss the die and then toss the coin. She wanted to know the probability that a 1 on the die and a head on the coin would appear. Emily knew that the "and" signal told her she must multiply. Show Emily how to find the probability that a one on the die and a head on the coin will appear.

_____

6.

a. Emily and four of her classmates are running to be class officers. Emily's classmates are Anjuli, Missa, Sarah, and Nina. There will be two class officers elected. The one who receives the most votes will be president. The individual who receives the second highest number of votes will be vice president. If Nina is elected president, which classmates might be elected vice president? Write their names in the blanks below the word "vice president" below.

President	Vice president
	_____
Nina	_____
	_____
	_____

b. If Anjuli is elected president, which classmates might be elected vice president? Write their names in the blanks below the word "vice president" below.

President	Vice president
	_____
Anjuli	_____
	_____
	_____

c. In the next exercise there are four possible candidates for three offices. The offices are president, vice president, and secretary. After the president and vice president are elected, the individual who receives the third highest number of votes will be secretary. The diagram below shows that Missa is elected president. Either Emily, Anjuli, or Sarah is elected vice president. Fill in the blanks in the diagram below that show the possible combinations of president, vice president, and secretary that could occur.

President	Vice president	Secretary
	_____	_____ or _____
Missa	_____	_____ or _____
	_____	_____ or _____

Name:_____ Date: _____

 Helping Emily Solve Problems (cont.)

7. Emily and her friends are going to fix tacos for lunch. She and her friends all like tacos, but they like different dressings and foods to place on the tacos. The diagram below, a taco tree, shows all of the different items that could be placed on the tacos. The dressing choices are salsa, sour cream, and cheese. Other food items available are lettuce, tomatoes, and jalapeños.

In the diagram below, place the choices on the correct blanks below the proper headings.

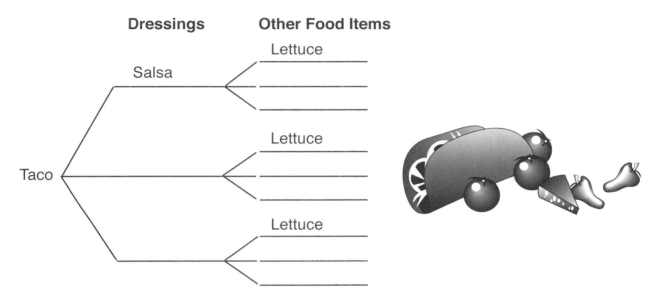

Answer the following questions. Assume that you can only pick one topping from each category for each taco.

a. How many taco choices can be made with different dressings only? _____

b. How many taco choices can be made with the dressings and lettuce? _____

c. How many taco choices can be made with the dressings, lettuce, and tomatoes? _____

d. How many taco choices can be made with dressings, lettuce, tomatoes, and jalapeños?

_____

e. Emily and her friends can make _____ different taco choices.

One of Emily's friends suggested that in addition to lettuce, tomatoes, and jalapeños, refried beans should be offered.

f. If refried beans are added to the choices, there will be _____ different taco choices.

Name:_____ Date: _____

  # Probability of an Event Not Happening

Emily was thinking about the probability problems that she had worked in class. She thought about the fact that if a die is tossed, the probability of the die landing with a 6 showing is $\frac{1}{6}$. She wondered what the probability was that a 1 would not appear. Emily remembered that the answer to probability problems was 0, 1, or a proper fraction between 0 and 1. Emily made the chart below to try to find the answer when a die is tossed. Help Emily fill in the blanks to find the answer.

 1.

Numbers on die	Probability that the number will appear		Probability that the number won't appear	
1	$\frac{1}{6}$	+	_____	= 1
2	$\frac{1}{6}$	+	_____	= 1
3	$\frac{1}{6}$	+	_____	= 1
4	$\frac{1}{6}$	+	_____	= 1
5	$\frac{1}{6}$	+	_____	= 1
6	$\frac{1}{6}$	+	_____	= 1

Answer the following questions.

2. When a coin is tossed, the probability that it will not land heads up is _____.

3. When a coin is tossed, the probability that it will not land tails up is _____.

A bag contains one white and two green marbles. A marble is drawn from the bag.

4. The probability that a white marble will be drawn is _____.

5. The probability that a white marble will not be drawn is _____.

A green marble is drawn from the bag and not replaced. A marble is then drawn from the bag.

6. The probability that a white marble will be drawn is _____.

7. The probability that a white marble will not be drawn is _____.

Name:_____ Date: _____

Statistics: Using a Frequency Distribution

Statistics is becoming a very important part of mathematics in today's world. It is the kind of mathematics that teaches us how to collect, organize, and understand number data. When you figure the average grade in a course or the average number of points scored by the basketball team, you are using statistics. Statistics has always been very useful in the study of science. Today the ability to use statistics is becoming important in many everyday jobs.

In statistics, collecting, organizing, and interpreting data is very important. To organize and interpret the data, different kinds of charts, graphs, and diagrams are used.

One very important tool for organizing and interpreting data is the **frequency distribution**. When a frequency distribution is used, the data is grouped so that it is easier to see the relationships among the data.

Developing a Frequency Distribution

Each of the following numbers represents the height in inches of one of the fourteen members of a basketball squad.

60, 65, 71, 64, 66, 68, 63, 65, 66, 62, 67, 75, 65, 66

Step 1: Arrange the numbers in a vertical column from largest to smallest under the height column in the diagram at right. The first number has been listed.

Step 2: Once the numbers are arranged in a vertical column under the height column, the heights must be tallied. Each time a number occurs, place a tally mark (I) next to the number in the tally column. The first one has been completed.

Step 3: After the tallies have all been recorded, total the number of tallies on each line. Place this number on the blank under the frequency column. The first one has been completed.

Height Column	Tally Column	Frequency Column
75	I	1
Totals:		

Directions: Answer the following.

1. The number(s) with the greatest number of tally marks is/are _____.

2. The number of tally marks for the number 65 is _____.

3. The total number of tally marks under the tally column is _____.

4. The sum of the numbers under the frequency column is _____.

Name:_____ Date: _____

Frequency Distributions Using Intervals

A **frequency distribution** is developed so that a pattern of numbers can be observed. When building a frequency distribution from a large group of numbers, it is often necessary to group the numbers into intervals. Then each of the numbers in the group is tallied in the interval containing that number.

Directions: The following exercise will help you understand how a frequency distribution is developed using intervals. Tally the following numbers in the interval where the number occurs. The first one (7) has been tallied in the interval 0–9 since the 7 is between 0 and 9.

25, 11, 34, 20, 22, 10, 18, 29, 44, 53, 16, 38, 26, 7, 49, 32, 21, 28, 35, 19

Number Interval	Tally	Frequency
50–59		
40–49		
30–39		
20–29		
10–19		
0–9	I	1
Totals:		

Directions: Answer the following questions.

1. The number of tallies in the interval 10–19 is _____.

2. The number of tallies in the interval 30–39 is _____.

3. The interval with the highest number of tallies is _____.

4. The interval length of the interval 10–19 is the number _____.

5. The interval length of the interval 40–49 is the number _____.

6. The interval length of each interval is the number _____.

7. In a frequency distribution, the interval lengths will all be the same _____.

In a frequency distribution using intervals, the smaller number on each interval is called the lower limit of that interval.

8. The number representing the lower limit of the interval 0–9 is [zero/nine].

9. The number representing the lower limit of the interval 20–29 is _____.

10. The number representing the lower limit of the interval 30–39 is _____.

11. In a frequency distribution, the intervals must all be _____ in length.

Frequency Distributions Using Intervals (cont.)

12. Complete the following blanks with multiples of the number on the first blank.

2 _____ _____ 8 _____ _____ _____ _____

13. Complete the following blanks with multiples of the number on the first blank.

5 _____ _____ _____ _____ 30 _____ _____ _____ _____

14. Complete the following blanks with multiples of the number on the first blank.

3 _____ _____ _____ 15 _____ _____ _____

15. In the frequency distribution on page 48, the numbers found on the lower limit of each interval are all multiples of the number _____.

16. In a frequency distribution, all lower limit numbers must be _____ of some number.

The eighth grade class took a twenty-word spelling test. The following are the number of words spelled correctly by the class.

12, 18, 7, 15, 19, 10, 11, 12, 13, 14, 16, 17, 15, 9, 10, 15, 15,13, 14, 18, 19, 16, 20, 18, 13, 15

Directions: Use the chart below and develop a frequency distribution for the above class scores. Use lengths of three. The first interval has been placed on the chart.

Interval Scores	Tally	Frequency
0–2		
Totals:		

Directions: Answer the following questions.

17. The lower limit numbers are 0 _____ _____ _____ _____ _____ _____.

18. The interval with the greatest number of tallies is the interval _____.

19. The interval length is the number _____.

20. The lower limit numbers are multiples of _____.

Name:_____   Date: _____

Developing a Frequency Polygon

The data from a frequency distribution is often used to develop a frequency polygon. A **frequency polygon** is a line graph used to show the shape or pattern of scores in a frequency distribution.

Directions: Develop a frequency polygon using the following data and following the steps below. Use the graphed diagram to develop the frequency polygon.

1, 3, 5, 7, 5, 6, 7, 6, 4, 5, 9, 6, 5, 7, 6, 4, 3, 5, 2, 8, 5

Step 1: Determine the range of scores in the data. The range is found by subtracting the smallest number in the group from the largest number in the group. Fill in the blanks to find the range.

a. ___ - ___ = ___   **b.** Range of above scores = ___.

Step 2: On the graphed chart below, choose a convenient scale for the horizontal axis. The horizontal axis is read from left to right. Let each rectangle on the horizontal axis equal 1. The horizontal axis will read from 0 on the left to 10 on the right. Complete the numbering of the horizontal axis at this time. Label the horizontal axis as the Scores.

Step 3: The length of the vertical axis should be approximately $\frac{2}{3}$ to $\frac{3}{4}$ the length of the horizontal axis. Since the horizontal axis is 10 equal-sized rectangles, use $\frac{3}{4}$ to find the length of the vertical axis.

a. $\frac{3}{4}$ of 10 = _____.

b. Round to the next highest whole number _____. The vertical axis will read from 0 at the bottom to that number at the top.

c. Complete the numbering of the vertical axis.

Step 4: Label the vertical axis to record the frequency of the scores in the data. (Frequency of scores.)

Step 5: Place a dot above each score on the horizontal axis that marks the frequency of the score.

Step 6: Start at the *x* on the horizontal line and connect the dots with a line. Bring the line down to the horizontal line at point *y*. In a frequency polygon, the line is always closed on each end.

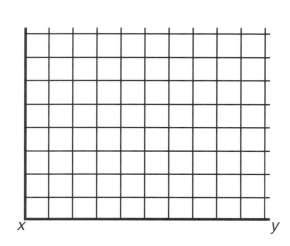

Name:_____ Date: _____

Stem and Leaf Plots

Another way of analyzing data is with a stem and leaf plot. The **stem and leaf plot** is unique in that all of the data is included.

The development of a stem and leaf plot begins with a T-Chart. The T-Chart is first labeled appropriately with the terms "stem" and "leaf." Each of the numbers in a group of data will appear in the T-Chart. Each number will be divided so that part of the number is the stem and the other part is the leaf. Then the stem part of the number will be recorded under "stem" on the T-Chart, and the other part of the number will be recorded under "leaf" on the T-Chart.

The T-Chart below has been developed using the numbers 188, 176, and 178. It is first necessary to determine the stem value. In the T-Chart below, the stem value represents the hundreds and tens places in each number. The ones value for each number is under the leaf part of the T-Chart.

Stem	Leaf
18	8
17	68

The 18 under "Stem" equals 180.
The 8 under "leaf" equals 8 ones.
The number is read 188.

The 17 under "Stem" equals 170.
The 6 under "leaf" equals 6 ones.
The number is read 176.
The 8 under "leaf" equals 8 ones.
The number is read 178.

Directions: Refer to the stem and leaf plot below and answer the questions that follow.

Stem	Leaf
13	4
14	0678
15	259

1. The 13 under the stem is the number _____.

2. The 14 under the stem is the number _____.

3. The 15 under the stem is the number _____.

4. The number represented by 13 under stem and 4 under leaf is the number _____.

5. The number represented by 14 under stem and 0 under leaf is the number _____.

6. The number represented by 14 under stem and 6 under leaf is the number _____.

7. The number represented by 14 under stem and 7 under leaf is the number _____.

8. The number represented by 14 under stem and 8 under leaf is the number _____.

9. In the stem and leaf T-Chart above, there are _____ numbers represented.

Name:_____ Date: _____

Stem and Leaf Plots (cont.)

Directions: The following numbers represent the number of free throws made by members of the girl's junior high basketball team during their seventh and eighth grade years. Develop a stem and leaf plot to show the free-throw data.

10. Use the following steps in developing the stem and leaf plot on the T-Chart below.
Step 1: Determine the value that the stem will represent.
Step 2: Write the stem values in order from smallest to largest below the stem column.
Step 3: Determine the value the leaf will represent.
Step 4: Order the leaf values for each stem value from smallest to largest.
Step 5: Write the leaf values for each stem in order from left to right next to the stem value with which the leaf belongs.

25, 11, 34, 20, 22, 10, 8, 29, 44, 53, 16, 38, 26, 7, 49, 32, 21, 28, 35, 19

Stem | Leaf

Answer the following questions:

a. The stem value 20 represents the numbers

____ ____ ____ ____ ____ ____ ____.

b. The stem value 30 represents the numbers

____ ____ ____ ____.

c. The stem value representing only one number is _____.

d. The stem value representing the most numbers is _____.

11. The numbers below represent the weights of the junior high football team. Use the T-Chart below and complete a stem and leaf plot that shows each of their weights.

118, 115, 125, 160, 90, 136, 138, 122, 167, 139, 94, 108, 138, 145, 154, 102, 141, 159, 158, 107, 155, 128, 129, 134, 133

Stem | Leaf

Refer to the stem and leaf plot at left and answer the following questions.

a. The number of football players weighing between 120 and 129 is _____.

b. The number of football players weighing between 150 and 159 is _____.

c. The number of football players weighing between 140 and 149 is _____.

d. The greatest number of football players recorded on the T-Chart for any stem number is _____.

Name:_____ Date: _____

Understanding Mean, Median, and Mode

Three very important terms in statistics are the *mean, median, and mode*. They are all measures of **central tendency** for a group of numbers. All of these can be used to find the average number when applied to a group of numbers. However, each of these terms will give you a different kind of average for the same group of numbers. Before finding out when to use each of these averages, it is important to know what each means and how to find it.

Mean

The **mean** of a group of numbers is found by finding the sum of a group of numbers and dividing the sum by how many numbers there are in the group. For example, the following are the scores of a student on five math tests: Test I: 60, Test II: 70, Test III: 80, Test IV: 85, Test V: 90. To find the mean of the scores, it is necessary to complete the following steps.

Step 1: Find the sum of the five scores.

   $60 + 70 + 80 + 85 + 90 = 385$

Step 2: Divide the sum by how many numbers were added.

   $385 \div 5 =$

Directions: Answer the following questions.

1. The sum of the five test scores is the number _____.

2. To find the mean, the sum is divided by _____.

3. The mean of the five math scores is _____.

In statistics, a special formula is used to find the mean of a group of numbers. The formula is $\bar{x} = \sum \div N$.

   $\bar{x}$ is used to indicate that the mean is to be found.
   $\sum$ is the numbers in the group added (the sum).
   N is the total number in the group.

For example, substitute the data for finding the mean of the five math test scores in the formula

   $\bar{x} = 77$ $\sum = 385$ $N = 5$ $77 = 385 \div 5$

Name:_____ Date: _____

Understanding Mean, Median, and Mode (cont.)

Directions: Find the mean of the following problems.

4. 50, 80, 60, 100, 70, 55, 75

    a. Step 1: ___ + ___ + ___ + ___ + ___ + ___ + ___ = ___ (Σ)

    b. Step 2: ___ (Σ) ÷ ___ (N) = ___ ($\overline{x}$)

    c. Step 3: $\overline{x}$ = ___

5. 90, 95, 60, 70, 85, 90, 80, 75, 65, 60

    a. Step 1: ___ + ___ + ___ + ___ + ___ + ___ + ___ + ___ + ___ + ___ = ___

    b. Step 2: ___ (Σ) ÷ ___ (N) = ___ ($\overline{x}$)

    c. Step 3: $\overline{x}$ = ___

6. 15, 10, 20, 25, 30, 10, 35, 40

    a. The sum is ___.

    b. The number of scores is ___.

    c. The sum divided by the number of scores is ___.

    d. The mean is ___.

Directions: Substitute the numbers given into the formula and find the mean.

7. Σ = 120 N = 10 $\Sigma \div N = \overline{x}$ ___ ÷ ___ = ___

8. Σ = 48 N = 6 $\Sigma \div N = \overline{x}$ ___ ÷ ___ = ___

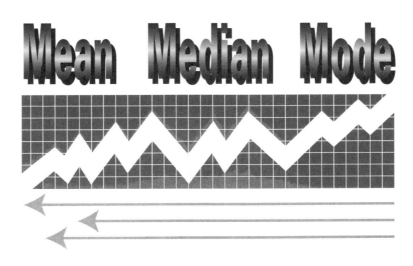

Understanding Mean, Median, and Mode (cont.)

Median

The **median** is often used in statistics. It is the number that is in the exact middle of a group of numbers. When the median number (middle) is found, one-half of the numbers will be above the median and one-half of the numbers below the median. Let's find the median of the five math test scores: 68, 75, 80, 90, and 85.

Step 1: Arrange the scores in order from largest at the top to smallest at the bottom in column form.

Step 2: Count from the top or bottom score until the score in the exact middle is found. Exactly one-half of the remaining scores will be above and below the median (middle) score.

Step 1: Five math scores in column form
90
85
80
75
68
Step 2: The median score for this group is 80.

Directions: Find the median for the following problems. Arrange the numbers in column form along the side of this page or on your own paper.

1. 5, 14, 7, 10, 9, 3, 18

   a. Arrange the numbers in order from largest to smallest in column form.

   b. The number in the median (middle) position is _____.

   c. The numbers above the median are _____, _____, and _____.

   d. The numbers below the median are _____, _____, and _____.

   e. One-_____ of the numbers in the group are above the median, and _____-half are below the median.

2. 50, 70, 40, 60, 75, 45, 90, 85, 65

   a. There are _____ numbers in the group.

   b. There will be _____ numbers above the median and _____ numbers below the median.

   c. The median number is _____.

   d. The numbers below the median are _____, _____, _____, and _____.

   e. The numbers above the median are _____, _____, _____, and _____.

3. 35, 18, 23, 12, 167, 65, 180, 32, 77, 900, 94, 25, 569, 87, 7

   a. There are _____ numbers in the group.

   b. The median number is _____.

Name:_____ Date: _____

Understanding Mean, Median, and Mode (cont.)

Mode

The **mode** is the number in a group that occurs most often. For example, in the group of numbers 3, 8, 4, 7, 3, 9, 4, 7, 3, 2, 5, 3, the number 3 occurs four times. This is more often than any other number; therefore, 3 would be the mode in this instance.

Directions: Find the mode in each of the following groups of numbers.

1. 9, 4, 6, 1, 5, 7, 9, 3, 2, 9

    a. The number ____ occurs most often in the group.

    b. The mode is the number ____.

2. 23, 56, 34, 89, 12, 56, 67

    a. The number _____ occurs most often in the group.

    b. The mode is the number _____.

3. 89, 12, 34, 78, 2, 8, 14, 35, 89, 14, 78, 14, 78, 90, 14, 78, 123, 89

    a. The greatest number of times any number occurs is _____.

    b. What number(s) occur(s) the greatest number of times? _____

If a group of numbers has different numbers that occur most often and the same number of times, there is more than one mode. If there are two different numbers that occur most often and the same number of times, the group of numbers is *bimodal.*

    c. The two modes in group #3 are the numbers _____ and _____.

    d. There are two modes, so the group of numbers is _____.

Review and Practice Lesson 6

The mean, median, and mode are all ways of looking at a group of numbers to determine which number(s) best represents the total group. In statistics, you are often trying to find a number that best tells you what the total group is like. The mean, median, and mode can all be used. However, for one group of numbers the mean may be best. For another group, the median may be best. The mode is sometimes best, although not as often.

The mean, median, and mode are all measures of central tendency for a group of numbers. The mean is the average number of a group. The median is the middle number of a group of numbers. The mode is the number(s) in a group that occurs most often.

Directions: Diagrams can often help you understand and remember what you have read. Refer to the two paragraphs above and fill in the rectangles in the diagram below. Use the following words or phrases in the rectangles.

Mean
Mode
Measures of central tendency
Most frequent number
Median
Average number
Middle number

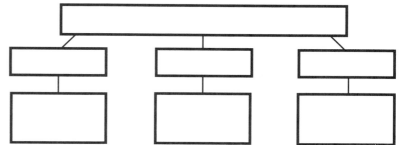

Tasha and her friends were going to give a report to help the class decide how much money the class must make to buy pizza for a class party. They called nine pizza places to find the prices for 16-inch pizzas. In their report, they could use only one amount to help the class make a decision about how much money must be earned.

The following are the nine prices that were given to them: $11.50, $6.75, $8.25, $7.00, $7.25, $8.00, $7.50, $7.75, $11.50.

They knew that they must give the class a cost figure that best represented the nine different prices. They decided to figure the mean, median, and mode for the nine pizza prices and then make a decision about which figure to use.

Directions: Find the mean, median, and mode for the pizza prices above.

1. Mean = $_____.   **2.** Median = $_____.   **3.** Mode = $_____.

4. Explain why the mode is so much higher than the mean or median. _____

_____

5. The difference in price between the mean and median is $ _____.

6. Find the mean and median of the pizzas leaving out the two prices of $11.50.

   a. Mean = $_____   **b.** Median = $_____

7. Explain why the mean and median prices are so different when the prices from the nine

   pizza places are used. _____

_____

Name:_____ Date: _____

Measures of Variability: Range

You have just completed a study of the measures of central tendency. Measures of variability are also important in statistics. The measures of **variability** are the **range** and **standard deviation**. These statistical procedures measure the way numbers scatter or vary.

The **range** is the difference between the highest and lowest numbers in a group of numbers. It is a very crude measure of variability and is seldom used for making decisions in statistical problems. The range is typically used to compare such things as the difference in temperature between the warmest and coldest days of the year, the warmest and coldest temperature of the month, or the warmest and coldest temperature of a day.

The **standard deviation** is a very important measure of variability. It is useful in making decisions that relate to solving problems in science and industry. The standard deviation is the measure of the variability that shows how numbers scatter around the mean. In other words, how variable are the numbers in a group from the mean?

Understanding the Range

Example: Scores are 2, 6, 7, 3, 9, 10, 23, 1, 8, 28.

Formula: High score − low score = range (H − L = R).

Highest score = 28, Lowest score = 1, Range = 27

Directions: Find the range for each of the following group of numbers.

1. 24, 10, 58, 89, 98, 13   _____ (H) − _____ (L) = _____ (R)

2. 234, 123, 456, 678, 278, 890   _____ (H) − _____ (L) = _____ (R)

3. 10, 45, 78, 46, 13, 65   _____ (H) − _____ (L) = _____ (R)

4. 245, 341, 256, 578, 765   _____ (H) − _____ (L) = _____ (R)

Directions: Complete the following.

5. The high and low temperatures in Phoenix, Arizona, for a 24-hour period were 73° and 45°. The range of temperatures for the 24-hour period was _____.

6. The highest and lowest daily sales for a pet shop for a seven-day period were $345.35 and $246.89. The range of sales for the seven-day period was _____.

7. The heights (in inches) of ten junior high basketball players are 56, 67, 58, 60, 58, 63, 62, 66, 55, and 61. The range is _____ inches.

Name:_____ Date: _____

Measures of Variability: Standard Deviation

The **standard deviation** is used to tell how scores scatter around the mean. The smaller the standard deviation, the more closely the scores cluster around the mean. When the standard deviation is large, the scores are more widely scattered.

Directions: Follow the steps to find the standard deviation.

The junior high baseball team played ten baseball games. Find the standard deviation for the runs scored by the team for the ten games. 5, 1, 5, 6, 7, 7, 2, 4, 8, 5

Step 1: Arrange the scores in order from smallest to largest in the blanks below and in the score column in the chart on the next page. Two have been completed. Find the sum of the scores.

A. ___ + ___ + ___ + ___ + ___ + ___ + ___ + ___ + ___ + ___ = _____

B. Divide the sum by the number of scores added to find the mean. _____

C. Another name for the mean is _____.

D. Place the answers for A and B on the chart on the next page in the blanks labeled A and B below the score column.

Step 2: Subtract the mean from each of the scores. Record the difference in the blanks under the Difference from Mean column. Two have been completed. Place the appropriate + or – sign in front of the number recorded under the Difference from Mean column.

Step 3: Find the square of each of the numbers recorded under the Difference from Mean column. Place the square in the blank under the Square of Difference column. Two have been completed.

Step 4: Find the sum of the numbers recorded under the Square of Difference column. The sum is _____. Record this answer in the blank labeled "C" under the Square of Difference column.

Step 5: The number of scores is _____. Record this answer in the blank labeled "D" under the Square of Difference column. Divide the sum found in Step 4 by the number of scores "D". Record this answer of "C divided by D" (rounded to the nearest whole number) in the blank labeled "E" under the Square of Difference column.

Step 6: Find the square root of the number recorded in "E". Record the answer in the blank labeled "F". This is the standard deviation of the 10 baseball scores.

Name:_____ Date: _____

Measures of Variability: Standard Deviation (cont.)

Score	Difference from Mean	Square of Difference
4	-1	1
7	+2	4

A. Sum = _____

B. Mean = _____

C. Sum = _____

D. Number = _____

(round) **E.** Mean (C ÷ D) = _____

F. Square root = _____

1. The answer in "F" rounded to the nearest whole number is _____.

Directions: Before answering the questions that follow, check the answer to Question 1 above.

When working with standard deviations, the reference point is always the mean of the data you are using.

2. The mean found in the above exercise is recorded in "B" under the "Score" column. The mean recorded in "B" is _____.

The term *+1 standard deviation* is read "Plus one standard deviation above the mean." To find the score that is +1 standard deviation of the mean, add the standard deviation found in "F" (rounded) to the mean found in "B" below the "Score" column. The number found is read "+1 standard deviation above the mean."

3. The standard deviation recorded in "F" above under the Square of the Difference column is the number (rounded) _____. Fill in the blanks below to find the number that is +1 standard deviation above the mean. Remember: mean + standard deviation = +1 standard deviation above the mean.   _____ + _____ = _____

Name:_____ Date: _____

░▒▓ Measures of Variability: Standard Deviation (cont.) ▓▒░

4. The term *-1 standard deviation* is read "minus one standard deviation below the mean."

To find the score that is -1 standard deviation, subtract the standard deviation found in "F" (rounded) from the mean found in "B" below the Score column.

Mean - standard deviation = -1 standard deviation below the mean. _____ – _____ = _____

Directions: Refer to the baseball scores in the chart on page 60 and answer the following questions.

5. List the three scores that are within +1 standard deviation of the mean. _____

6. List the one score that is within -1 standard deviation of the mean. _____

7. The scores that are between -1 and +1 standard deviations of the mean are _____

_____

Review and Practice

1. The range and standard deviation are measures of _____.

2. The standard deviation is used to find the variability or how the numbers in a group

_____ around the _____.

3. Find the standard deviation for the following data. Use the chart below to record the steps.

80, 100, 92, 90, 96, 94

Scores	Difference from Mean	Square of Difference

A. Sum _____   **C.** Sum _____

B. Mean _____   (rounded)   **D.** Mean _____

Standard deviation = square root of "D"

E. Standard deviation = _____ (rounded to whole number)

Name:_____ Date: _____

Practical Applications for Standard Deviation

Standard deviation is often used by manufacturers. It is used to make sure the product produced meets the standards necessary for the product to be purchased. There will always be some items that do not meet the required standard. However, the manufacturer must make sure that the number not meeting the standard is very small.

Baseballs must be nine inches in circumference. Any baseball that was less than $8\frac{7}{8}$ inches or more than $9\frac{1}{8}$ inches would have to be sold at a reduced price. The manufacturer decided that 1,000 new balls would be measured. Every tenth ball made was selected for measurement. The balls were measured, and the mean circumference was found. The standard deviation was found to be $\frac{1}{8}$ inch. The following chart shows the results of measuring the 1,000 selected baseballs.

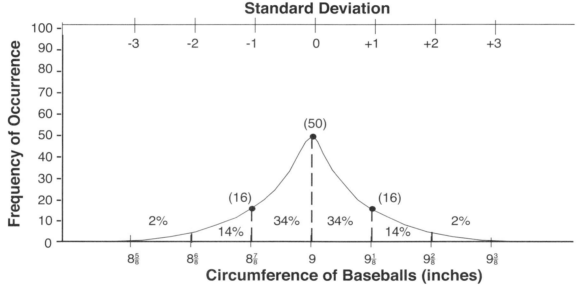

Directions: Answer the following questions.

1. The mean circumference of the 1,000 baseballs is _____ inches.

2. What percent of the baseballs were within +1 standard deviation of the mean? _____

3. What percent of the baseballs were within -1 standard deviation of the mean? _____

4. What percent of the baseballs were within +1 and -1 standard deviation of the mean? _____

5. What percent of the baseballs were within +2 standard deviation of the mean? _____

6. What percent of the baseballs were within -2 standard deviation of the mean? _____

7. What percent of the baseballs were within +2 and -2 standard deviation of the mean? _____

8. What percent of the baseballs were within +3 and -3 standard deviation of the mean? _____

9. How many of the 1,000 baseballs are less than $8\frac{7}{8}$ inches in circumference? _____

10. How many of the 1,000 baseballs must be sold at a reduced price? _____

Name:_____ Date: _____

Understanding Correlation

You have learned that in the study of statistics, the use of charts, graphs, stem and leaf diagrams, and frequency distributions are very important. Such tools are important because they help organize the data that is studied.

Correlation is a term that is very common in statistics. **Correlation** is used when we want to know if one set of data is related to another set of data. For example, is the percent of free throws made related to the height of the player?

Correlations between sets of data may show a positive relationship, a negative relationship, or no relationship at all. A **positive relationship** exists if an increase in one set of data results in an increase in the other set of data. A **negative relationship** exists if an increase in one set of data results in a decrease in the other set of data.

After the two sets of data have been plotted on the correlation diagram, an inspection of the dots for patterns is necessary. The three patterns that you will look for in the exercises that follow are illustrated in A, B, and C below.

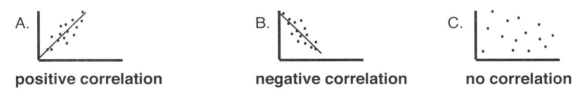

A. **positive correlation** B. **negative correlation** C. **no correlation**

The study of correlation will begin with the comparison of two sets of data for 15 members of the junior high basketball squad. One set of data will be the percent of free throws made by each of the squad members. The other set of data will be the height of each of the squad members. The question is: Is there a relationship between the percent of free throws made and height?

The chart below lists the players, the percent of free throws made, and their heights.

Squad Member	Percent of Free Throws Made	Height (inches)
A	75	60
B	45	62
C	35	58
D	60	65
E	30	63
F	90	58
G	25	63
H	85	62
I	45	63
J	50	60
K	90	66
L	20	59
M	10	60
N	80	58
O	40	67

Name:_____ Date: _____

Understanding Correlation (cont.)

The sets of data on the previous page will be recorded on the diagram below. For each player a dot will be used to locate the point on the diagram where the player's percent of free throws made and height meet.

The location of the dot is found by extending a horizontal line to the right from the height of each player. Next, a vertical line is extended upward from the percent of free throws made on the base of the diagram. For each player, the point where the two lines cross is marked with a dot. The dot for player A has been located on the diagram.

Directions: Complete the diagram by locating a dot on the diagram for each of the players in the chart on page 63. When you have placed the 15 dots on the diagram, you will have plotted a correlation diagram. The diagram can help you determine if a correlation exists between the two sets of data.

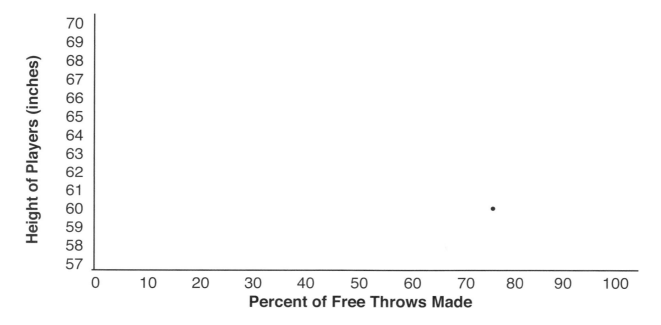

Directions: Circle the correct answers to the following questions.

1. The pattern of dots in the above correlation diagram most closely matches the pattern for

   a) positive correlation   b) negative correlation   c) no correlation

2. The taller a player is, the better the percent of free throws made.   a) true   b) false

Name:_____ Date: _____

Finding Correlation in Test Scores

The following are two sets of data for an eighth grade class. One set of data is the mathematics test scores for each student. The other set of data is the time each student spent studying for the test. The question is: Is there a correlation between the two sets of data?

Directions: The mathematics test score for each student is listed below. The time spent studying is in parenthesis next to the student score. Plot these two sets of data for each student on the correlation diagram below. (A, B, C, and D on the graph will be used in the exercise that follows.)

60 (15), 80 (20), 40 (5), 50 (10), 90 (60), 30 (10), 75 (40), 95 (45), 100 (45), 45 (5), 55 (20), 35 (5), 85 (35), 80 (30), 90 (35), 50 (10), 20 (5), 100 (50), 70 (20), 75 (25), 85 (35), 70 (25), 85 (40), 80 (35)

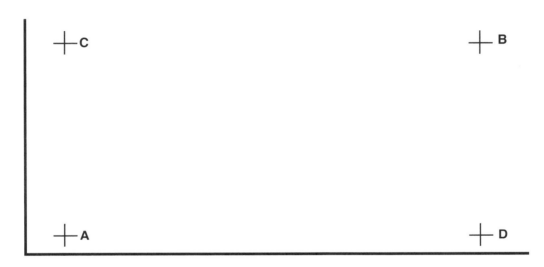

Directions: Complete the following using the diagram above.

1. Draw a line connecting points A and B.
2. Draw a line connecting points C and D.
3. Line A–B is [vertical, horizontal, diagonal].
4. Line C–D is [vertical, horizontal, diagonal].
5. The line indicating a trend that as one set of data increases the other set of data also increases is line _____.
6. The line indicating a trend that as one set of data increases the other set of data decreases is line _____.
7. In the correlation diagram above, the pattern of dots most closely matches line _____.
8. In the correlation diagram above, there appears to be a positive relationship between mathematics test _____ and time spent _____.

Name:_____ Date: _____

Finding Correlation in Test Scores (cont.)

Directions: The following math test scores were made by the members of an eighth-grade class. The test scores for each student and the heights of the student are listed below. The test score is listed with the height of the student, in inches, in parentheses. Plot the data and develop a scatter plot for math test score and height of the student making the score.

60 (63), 80 (65), 40 (69), 50 (70), 90 (62), 90 (67), 30 (61), 75 (62), 95 (66), 100 (64), 45 (64), 55 (68), 35 (67), 85 (72), 80 (65), 90 (60), 50 (67), 20 (61), 100 (71), 70 (73), 75 (65), 85 (66), 70 (60), 85 (60), 80 (66)

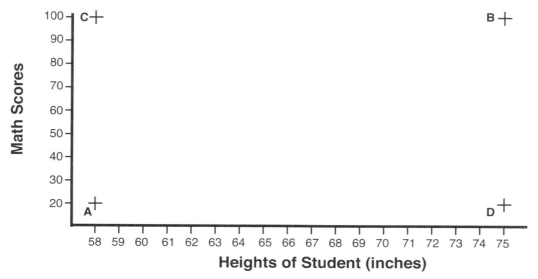

Directions: Complete the following corellation activities.

9. On each of the following graphs (9a, 9b, and 9c), select the appropriate scatterplot pattern (A, B, or C) that illustrates the correlation pattern listed under each graph. Then draw the illustration in A, B, or C on the appropriate graph.

9a. _____

9b. _____

9c. _____

Negative pattern

No pattern

Positive pattern

A.

B.

C.

Name:_____ Date: _____

Finding Correlation in Test Scores (cont.)

10. Match the pattern type in Column B with the description in Column A.

Column A   **Column B**

____ **a.** A high score in math is associated   **A.** A negative pattern of dots on the
with an increased amount of time   scatterplot.
spent studying.

____ **b.** A low score in math is associated   **B.** A positive pattern of dots on the
with an increased amount of time   scatterplot.
spent watching television.

____ **c.** A high score in math is associated   **C.** A pattern of dots on the scatter plot
with the month in which the student   indicating no relationship between
was born.   the two sets of data.

11. Draw a line between points A and B on the scatterplot on page 66. Draw a line between points C and D. The pattern of dots plotted on the scatterplot (math scores and student height) indicates: (check one)

____ **a.** a pattern of dots along the line A–B indicating a positive relationship between math scores and student height.

____ **b.** a pattern of dots along the line C–D indicating a negative relationship between math scores and student height.

____ **c.** no pattern exists, so there is no relationship between the math score made and student height.

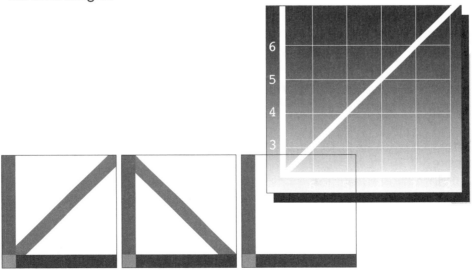

Review and Practice Lesson 7: Matching

Directions: Place the letter of the term in Column B that corresponds with the statement in Column A on the line next to that statement.

Column A

_____ **1.** A crude measure of variability.

_____ **2.** The measure of central tendency dividing the numbers so that 50 percent are above and 50 percent are below a given number.

_____ **3.** The measure of central tendency that identifies the most frequently appearing number.

_____ **4.** The range is one measure of variability. The other is . . .

_____ **5.** Refers to the relationship between two sets of data either positive, negative, or no relationship.

_____ **6.** Found by finding the sum of a group of numbers and dividing by the total numbers in the group.

_____ **7.** The mean, median, and mode are . . .

_____ **8.** The range and standard deviation are . . .

_____ **9.** When two sets of data increase together, the correlation is . . .

_____ **10.** When an increase in one set of data is marked with a decrease in the other set of data the correlation is . . .

Column B

A. Measures of Central Tendency

B. Mean

C. Correlation

D. Range

E. Mode

F. Standard Deviation

G. Positive

H. Median

I. Negative

J. Measures of Variability

Answer Keys

Understanding Proper Fractions (page 1)

1. 1   **2.** 2   **3.** 3   **4.** 4
5. 3   **6.** 3   **7.** 1   **8.** 7
9. 2   **10.** 5   **11.** 3   **12.** 3
13. 4   **14.** 5   **15.** 8   **16.** 5
17. 2   **18.** 8   **19.** 5   **20.** 6
21. numerator
22. denominator
23. smaller
24. a. $\frac{1}{3}$ b. $\frac{3}{8}$ c. $\frac{1}{2}$

Simplifying Proper Fractions (page 2)

1. $\frac{1}{3}$ **2.** $\frac{3}{5}$ **3.** $\frac{2}{3}$ **4.** $\frac{1}{2}$
5. $\frac{3}{4}$ **6.** $\frac{7}{8}$ **7.** $\frac{4}{5}$ **8.** $\frac{2}{5}$
9. $\frac{3}{4}$ **10.** $\frac{5}{7}$
11. $\frac{1}{5}; \frac{5}{5}; 1$ **12.** $\frac{1}{4}; \frac{4}{4}; 1$
13. $\frac{1}{3}; \frac{3}{3}; 1$ **14.** $\frac{1}{8}; \frac{8}{8}; 1$
15. $\frac{1}{2}; \frac{2}{2}; 1$ **16.** $\frac{1}{10}; \frac{10}{10}; 1$

Changing Proper Fractions to Decimals (page 3)

1. $1 \div 3 = 0.333 = 0.33$
2. $3 \div 5 = 0.6 = 0.60$
3. $2 \div 3 = 0.666 = 0.67$
4. $1 \div 2 = 0.5 = 0.50$
5. $3 \div 4 = 0.75 = 0.75$
6. $7 \div 8 = 0.875 = 0.88$
7. $4 \div 5 = 0.8 = 0.80$
8. $2 \div 5 = 0.4 = 0.40$
9. $3 \div 8 = 0.375 = 0.38$
10. $5 \div 6 = 0.833 = 0.83$

Changing Proper Fractions to Percents (page 4)

1. $1 \div 3 = 0.333 = 0.33 = 33\%$
2. $3 \div 5 = 0.6 = 0.60 = 60\%$
3. $2 \div 3 = 0.666 = 0.67 = 67\%$
4. $1 \div 2 = 0.5 = 0.50 = 50\%$
5. $3 \div 4 = 0.75 = 0.75 = 75\%$
6. $7 \div 8 = 0.875 = 0.88 = 88\%$
7. $4 \div 5 = 0.8 = 0.80 = 80\%$
8. $2 \div 5 = 0.4 = 0.40 = 40\%$
9. $3 \div 8 = 0.375 = 0.38 = 38\%$
10. $5 \div 6 = 0.833 = 0.83 = 83\%$

Probability of an Event (pages 5–6)

1. 1   **2.** heads, tails
3. $\frac{1}{2}$ **4.** $\frac{1}{2}$
5. $\frac{1}{2}$ **6.** 2
7. heads, tails   **8.** $\frac{1}{2}$
9. 4
10. heads heads; heads tails; tails heads; tails tails

probability tree: teacher check

Probability Ratios: Between 0 and 1 (pages 7–8)

1. 0   **2.** 1 or 100%
3. $\frac{1}{6}$ **4.** $\frac{1}{6}$
5. $\frac{1}{6}$ **6.** 1; 1; 1; 1; 1; 1; 1
7. 1   **8.** 0
9. proper fraction   **10.** $\frac{1}{4}$
11. $\frac{1}{4}$ **12.** $\frac{1}{4}$
13. $\frac{1}{4}$ **14.** 1; 1; 1; 1; 4
15. 1   **16.** 0
17. 0, 1   **18.** 1
19. 0   **20.** $\frac{1}{2}$
21. $\frac{1}{2}$ **22.** one
23. zero

Heads or Tails? (page 9)

1. 10   **2.** 6   **3.** 4   **4.** $\frac{6}{10}$
5. $\frac{3}{5}$ **6.** $\frac{4}{10}$ **7.** $\frac{2}{5}$ **8.** $\frac{3}{10}$
9. $\frac{7}{10}$ **10.** $\frac{8}{10}$ **11.** $\frac{2}{5}$ **12.** $\frac{4}{5}$

A Coin-Tossing Experiment (page 10)
Answers depend on student predictions and the outcome of the experiment.

How Many Outcomes? (page 11)
1. 2
2. head; tail
3. $\frac{1}{6}$; $\frac{1}{6}$; $\frac{1}{6}$; $\frac{1}{6}$; $\frac{1}{6}$; $\frac{1}{6}$; $\frac{6}{6}$; 1
4–5. Teacher check

A Die-Tossing Experiment (page 12)
Answers depend on student predictions and the outcomes of the experiment.

More Die-Tossing (page 13)
Answers depend on student predictions and the outcomes of the experiment.

Review and Practice Lesson 1 (page 14)
1. $\frac{1}{2}$; 0.50; 50%   2. $\frac{1}{2}$; 0.50; 50%
3. $\frac{2}{5}$; 0.40; 40%   4. $\frac{2}{3}$; 0.67; 67%
5. $\frac{4}{5}$; 0.80; 80%   6. $\frac{1}{3}$; 0.33; 33%
7. $\frac{3}{5}$; 0.60; 60%   8. $\frac{2}{3}$; 0.67; 67%
9. event
10. probability
11. two; outcomes
12. six; outcomes
13. proper
14. fraction
15. numerator; denominator
16. $\frac{1}{2}$ 17. $\frac{1}{6}$
18. $\frac{6}{6}$ 19. $\frac{0}{6}$
20. $\frac{2}{2}$ 21. $\frac{0}{2}$

Pick a Number (pages 16–17)
1. $\frac{1}{10}$ 2. 0.10
3. 10%   4. $\frac{10}{10}$; 1.0; 100%
5–6. Teacher check
7. $\frac{1}{40}$ 8. 0.025 or 0.03

9. 3%   10. $\frac{40}{40}$; 1.0; 100%
11. $\frac{1}{40}$; 0.03; 3%   12. $\frac{1}{40}$; 0.03; 3%
13. $\frac{10}{40}$; 0.25; 25%   14. $\frac{20}{40}$; 0.50; 50%
15. 0   16. 100

Review and Practice Lesson 2 (pages 18–20)
1. 2
2–6. Answers depend on the outcome of the experiment and student predictions.
7. event
8. heads; tails
9–10. Answers depend on the outcome of the experiment.
11. number
12–18. Answers depend on the outcome of the experiment and student predictions.
19. B
20. events; confidence; predictions

Population Sampling (pages 22–23)
1. the entire group of interest
2. part of an entire group of interest
3. that every member of the group is equally likely to be selected
4. sample
5. population
6. random
7. The coach should teach the free-throwing technique to the rest of the squad.

Sample Space (pages 24–25)
1. head; tail
2. 1, 3, 4, 5, 6
3. 1, 2, 3, 4, 5, 6, 7, 9, 10, 12
4. 10, 20, 30, 40, 50, 60, 70
5. 20

Marbles in a Bag
6. $\frac{1}{3}$; 0.33; 33%
7. $\frac{1}{3}$; 0.33; 33%

8. $\frac{1}{3}$; 0.33; 33%
9. 0
10. 100
11. population
12. sample
13. random sample
14. sample space

Sampling Practice (pages 27–28)
1. population
2. sample
3. random
4. 25
5. 25
6–10. Answers depend on the outcome of the experiment and student predictions.
11. A. 5; B. 10; C. 20
12. 130
13. 3
14. sample

Probability When Outcomes Are Not Equally Likely (pages 29–30)
1. $\frac{1}{5}$
2. $\frac{4}{5}$
3. 1 or 100%
4. 0 or 0%
5. $\frac{1}{5}$
6. $\frac{3}{5}$
7. $\frac{1}{5}$
8. $\frac{1}{5}$
9. $\frac{3}{5} + \frac{1}{5} + \frac{1}{5} = \frac{5}{5}$
10. 5
11. event
12. $\frac{1}{5}$
13. $\frac{3}{5}$
14. $\frac{1}{5}$
15. 12

16. event
17. $\frac{1}{12}$; $\frac{1}{12}$; 0.08; 8%
18. $\frac{3}{12}$; $\frac{1}{4}$; 0.25; 25%
19. $\frac{6}{12}$; $\frac{1}{2}$; 0.50; 50%
20. $\frac{2}{12}$; $\frac{1}{6}$; 0.17; 17%
21. 8 + 25 + 50 + 17 = 100

Probability: Going Around in Circles (page 31)
1. $\frac{1}{2}$
2. $\frac{1}{4}$
3. $\frac{1}{6}$
4. $\frac{1}{6}$
5. $\frac{2}{6}$ or $\frac{1}{3}$
6. $\frac{1}{6}$
7. D
8. D
9. C
10. B
11. A
12. C

Review and Practice Lesson 3 (page 32)
1. 20
2. event
3. $\frac{5}{20}$; $\frac{1}{4}$
4. 0.25
5. 25
6. $\frac{4}{20}$; $\frac{1}{5}$
7. 0.20
8. 20
9. $\frac{1}{20}$; $\frac{1}{20}$
10. 0.05
11. 5
12. 0; 1

Understanding Mutually Exclusive Events (page 33)
1. $\frac{1}{3}$ or $\frac{2}{6}$
2. $\frac{1}{3}$ or $\frac{2}{6}$
3. $\frac{1}{2}$ or $\frac{3}{6}$, 50
4. $\frac{2}{3}$ or $\frac{4}{6}$; 67
5. 2, 4, 6
6. $\frac{1}{2}$ or $\frac{3}{6}$; 50
7. 1, 3, 5
8. $\frac{1}{2}$ or $\frac{3}{6}$; 50
9. $\frac{6}{6}$, 100
10. $\frac{0}{6}$, 0

More Mutually Exclusive Events (page 34)

1. $\frac{1}{2}$ or $\frac{2}{4}$, 50
2. $\frac{1}{2}$ or $\frac{2}{4}$, 50
3. $\frac{3}{4}$, 75
4. green, red, black, white (any order)
5. $\frac{1}{2}$, $\frac{1}{2}$, $\frac{2}{2}$, 1
6. 40%
7. 20%
8. 40%
9. 60%
10. 80%

Independent Events (page 35)

1. $\frac{1}{6}$, $\frac{1}{6}$, $\frac{1}{36}$, 3
2. $\frac{1}{6}$, $\frac{1}{6}$, $\frac{1}{36}$, 3
3. $\frac{1}{6}$, $\frac{1}{6}$, $\frac{1}{6}$, $\frac{1}{216}$, 0.5
4. $\frac{1}{2}$, $\frac{1}{2}$, $\frac{1}{4}$, 25
5. $\frac{1}{2}$, $\frac{1}{2}$, $\frac{1}{4}$, 25
6. $\frac{1}{2}$, $\frac{1}{2}$, $\frac{1}{2}$, $\frac{1}{8}$, 13
7. $\frac{1}{2}$, $\frac{1}{2}$, $\frac{1}{2}$, $\frac{1}{2}$, $\frac{1}{16}$, 6
8. $\frac{1}{16}$, 6
9. $\frac{1}{16}$, 6
10. $\frac{1}{64}$, 2

Review and Practice Lesson 4 (page 36)

1. coin toss; 10; heads/tails; $\frac{1}{2}$
2. die toss; 20; 1/2/3/4/5/6; $\frac{1}{6}$
3. marble draw; 1; blue/red/black/green/white/orange; $\frac{1}{6}$
4. marble draw; 1; blue/red/black/green/white/orange; blue $\frac{1}{20}$; red $\frac{2}{20}$; black $\frac{3}{20}$; green $\frac{3}{20}$; white $\frac{5}{20}$; orange $\frac{6}{20}$
5. spinner; 1; 1/2/3/4/5/6; $\frac{1}{6}$
6. spinner; 1; red/blue/green/orange; $\frac{1}{4}$
7. spinner; 1; A/B/C/D/E/F/G/H; $\frac{1}{8}$

Dependent and Independent Events (page 37–38)

1. B
2. B
3. C
4. B
5. A
6. C
7. D
8. C
9. B
10. C
11. B
12. A
13. C
14. C
15. D
16. B
17. B
18. A
19. B
20. B
21. C
22. D
23. A
24. B
25. A
26. B

Revisiting Probability Trees (page 39)

1. 2
2. $\frac{3}{5}$
3. $\frac{3}{5}$
4. $\frac{3}{5}$
5. $\frac{2}{5}$
6. $\frac{2}{5}$
7. $\frac{2}{5}$
8. did not
9. 3
10. $\frac{2}{3}$
11. $\frac{1}{3}$
12. did

Learning More About Probability Trees (page 40)

1. Teacher check tree
2. 1C; 2A, 2B; 3A, 3B, 3C; 4A, 4C; 5A, 5B, 5C; 6B, 6C
3. 18
4. $\frac{1}{6}$
5. $\frac{1}{3}$
6. $\frac{1}{3}$ or $\frac{2}{6}$
7. $\frac{2}{3}$

Review and Practice Lesson 5: Crossword Puzzle (page 41)

Helping Emily Solve Problems (pages 42–45)

1. Emily. Though reasonably the next toss would result in a tail, the outcomes are independent.

2. She didn't toss the die enough times for the experiment to show the correct probability in general. The more times the die is tossed, the closer Emily's results will be to those that she read about.

3.

	G	W	R	B
1.	$\frac{15}{25}$	$\frac{5}{25}$	$\frac{4}{25}$	$\frac{1}{25}$
2.	$\frac{14}{24}$	$\frac{5}{24}$	$\frac{4}{24}$	$\frac{1}{24}$
3.	$\frac{13}{23}$	$\frac{5}{23}$	$\frac{4}{23}$	$\frac{1}{23}$
4.	$\frac{13}{22}$	$\frac{4}{22}$	$\frac{4}{22}$	$\frac{1}{22}$
5.	$\frac{13}{21}$	$\frac{4}{21}$	$\frac{3}{21}$	$\frac{1}{21}$
6.	$\frac{12}{20}$	$\frac{4}{20}$	$\frac{3}{20}$	$\frac{1}{20}$
7.	$\frac{12}{19}$	$\frac{3}{19}$	$\frac{3}{19}$	$\frac{1}{19}$
8.	$\frac{12}{18}$	$\frac{2}{18}$	$\frac{3}{18}$	$\frac{1}{18}$
9.	$\frac{12}{17}$	$\frac{2}{17}$	$\frac{2}{17}$	$\frac{1}{17}$
10.	$\frac{11}{16}$	$\frac{2}{16}$	$\frac{2}{16}$	$\frac{1}{16}$

4. $\frac{1}{6} + \frac{1}{2} = \frac{1}{6} + \frac{3}{6} = \frac{4}{6} = \frac{2}{3} = 67\%$

5. $\frac{1}{6} \times \frac{1}{2} = \frac{1}{12} = 8\%$

6. a. Anjuli, Missa, Sarah, Emily (any order)
   b. Missa, Emily, Sarah, Nina (any order)
   c.

VP	Secretary
Emily $\longrightarrow$	Anjuli or Sarah (any order)
Anjuli $\longrightarrow$	Sarah or Emily (any order)
Sarah $\longrightarrow$	Emily or Anjuli (any order)

   (any order)

7. Teacher check tree
   a. 3
   b. 3
   c. 6
   d. 9
   e. 9
   f. 12

Probability of an Event Not Happening (page 46)

1. $\frac{5}{6}; \frac{5}{6}; \frac{5}{6}; \frac{5}{6}; \frac{5}{6}; \frac{5}{6}$
2. $\frac{1}{2}$
3. $\frac{1}{2}$
4. $\frac{1}{3}$
5. $\frac{2}{3}$
6. $\frac{1}{2}$
7. $\frac{1}{2}$

Statistics: Using a Frequency Distribution (page 47)

Chart: Teacher check
1. 66 and 65
2. 3
3. 14
4. 14

Frequency Distributions Using Intervals (pages 48–49)

Charts: Teacher check.

1. 5
2. 4
3. 20–29
4. 10
5. 10
6. 10
7. number
8. zero
9. 20
10. 30
11. equal
12. 4, 6, 10, 12, 14, 16
13. 10, 15, 20, 25, 35, 40, 45, 50
14. 6, 9, 12, 18, 21, 24
15. 10
16. multiples
17. 3, 6, 9, 12, 15, 18
18. 15–17
19. 3
20. 3

Developing a Frequency Polygon (page 50)

Step 1: a. 9 - 1 = 8 **b.** 8
Step 3: a. 7.5   **b.** 8 **c.** Teacher check
Steps 4–6:

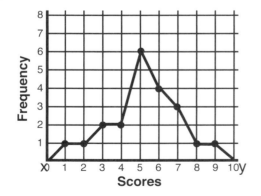

Stem and Leaf Plots (page 51–52)

1. 130
2. 140
3. 150
4. 134
5. 140
6. 146
7. 147
8. 148
9. 8
10.

Stem	Leaf
0	78
1	0169
2	0125689
3	2458
4	49
5	3

   a. 20, 21, 22, 25, 26, 28, 29
   b. 32, 34, 35, 38
   c. 50
   d. 20
11.

Stem	Leaf
9	04
10	278
11	58
12	2589
13	346889
14	15
15	4589
16	07

   a. 4
   b. 4
   c. 2
   d. 6

Understanding Mean, Median, and Mode (page 53–56)

Mean

1. 385
2. 5
3. 77
4. **a.** 490 ($\sum$) **b.** 490 ÷ 7 = 70   **c.** 70
5. **a.** 770 ($\sum$) **b.** 770 ÷ 10 = 77   **c.** 77

6. a. 185   **b.** 8   **c.** 23.125
    d. 23
7. 120 ÷ 10 = 12
8. 48 ÷ 6 = 8
Median
  1. a. 18, 14, 10, 9, 7, 5, 3
      b. 9
      c. 10, 14, 18
      d. 7, 5, 3
      e. half; one
  2. a. 9
      b. 4, 4
      c. 65
      d. 60, 50, 45, 40
      e. 70, 75, 85, 90
  3. a. 15
      b. 65

Mode
  1. a. 9   **b.** 9
  2. a. 56   **b.** 56
  3. a. 4   **b.** 14, 78
      c. 14, 78   **d.** bimodal

Review and Practice Lesson 6 (page 57)
Chart:

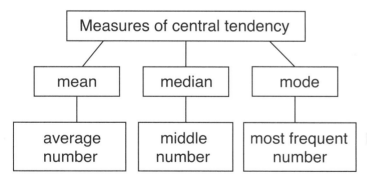

1. 8.39
2. 7.75
3. 11.50
4. The mode is the most often occuring number. The highest price occurred most often.
5. 0.64
6. a. 7.50   **b.** 7.50

7. The mean is influenced by the two extreme prices of 11.50, while the median is not influenced by the size of these two extreme prices.

Measures of Variability: Range (page 58)
  1. 98 - 10 = 88
  2. 890 - 123 = 767
  3. 78 - 10 = 68
  4. 765 - 245 = 520
  5. 28°
  6. $98.46
  7. 12

Measures of Variability: Standard Deviation (pages 59–61)
Step 1:
A. 1 + 2 + 4 + 5 + 5 + 5 + 6 + 7 + 7 + 8 = 50
B. 5
C. average
Step 4:   44
Step 5:   10
Chart:
A. 50   **B.** 5   **C.** 44   **D.** 10
E. 4   **F.** 2
  1. 2
  2. 5
  3. 2; 5 + 2 = 7
  4. 5 - 2 = 3
  5. 6, 7, 7
  6. 4
  7. 4, 5, 5, 5, 6, 7, 7

Review and Practice
  1. variability
  2. cluster; mean
  3. A. 552
      B. 92
      C. 232
      D. 39
      E. 6

Practical Applications for Standard Deviation (page 62)
1. 9
2. 34%
3. 34%
4. 68%
5. 48%
6. 48%
7. 96%
8. 100%
9. 160
10. 320

Understanding Correlation (page 64)
Diagram: Teacher check
1. c
2. b

Finding Correlation in Test Scores (pages 65–67)
1–2.   teacher check
3. diagonal
4. diagonal
5. A-B
6. C-D
7. A-B
8. scores, studying
9. **a.** C
   b. B
   c. A
10. **a.** B
    b. A
    c. C
11. c

Review and Practice Lesson 7: Matching (page 68)
1. D	2. H	3. E	4. F
5. C	6. B	7. A	8. J
9. G	10. I		